THE PORTLAND
BOTTOM LINE

Front cover design: Kelly Quashnie (Studio Cue, StudioCue.com)

Cover layout: Heather Schiffke (Cameron Design, CameronDesignPDX.com) and Jane Pellicciotto (Allegro Design, Allegro-Design.com)

Interior layout: Peter Korchnak (GoodBookery, GoodBookery.com)

Copy-editing: Mike Russell (Pivotal Writing, PivotalWriting.com) and Peter Korchnak

Published in Portland, Oregon, by GoodBookery with Lulu.

Printed in LaVergne, Tennessee, by Lightning Source, holder of Chain of Custody certifications from the Forest Stewardship Council (FSC®), Sustainable Forestry Initiative (SFI®), and Programme for the Endorsement of Forest Certification (PEFC™).

GoodBookery, LLC

P.O. Box 42111

Portland, OR 97242

U.S.A.

GoodBookery.com

First edition.

ISBN 978-0-9830467-0-7

Inside "The Portland Bottom Line"

To Portland, Oregon

Foreword: "Portland, Oregon? Why Would You Move There?"

Darcy Winslow

In 1986, I stunned my friends in Connecticut with the news that my husband and I would be moving back to our beloved Portland. They were incredulous that I would abandon "civilization" to return to the relative wilds and simplicity of a small, undeveloped town. In the 1980s, Portland was seen as an inconspicuous backwater between San Francisco and Seattle. Today, the response to, "Where do you live?", is equally filled with amazement, although for the complete opposite reason.

During the 1990s, I noticed a shift in peoples' reactions to Portland. Their response now came with a hint of "tree-hugger country", but with some decent music and food scenes emerging. While these reactions were no longer accented with disdain, voices still bore a hint of disregard.

Earlier this decade, the response began to change dramatically. Once, while on a business trip in New York City, a shop owner asked where I was from (obviously not Manhattan). Her response to "Portland" has since become emblematic of its growing reputation: "It was just written up in the *New York Times* as one of the most progressive and beautiful cities—I can't wait to visit!" I now get similar responses wherever I go—whether to Antarctica, Iceland, or Paris.

Today, I proudly expound on Portland's virtues and the steps we are taking as an engaged community to create a new future—a new reality, a new economy, but with our feet firmly planted in the need for global systemic change. Why the shift in attitude toward Portland?

There are many contributing factors: among them, visionary city and business leaders, as well as passionate, creative entrepreneurs—all working to improve our world through their business practices. These representatives of Portland's sustainable business ethos implicitly understand the symbiotic relationship between social responsibility, economic prosperity and environmental stewardship—and the quest for achieving a state of equilibrium.

The ideas shared in the following pages have been tested and proven in the crucible of the local economy. They are both a milestone of achievement and a platform from which to refine and launch even more ambitious projects. Portland has stepped up to redefine what "business as usual" can accomplish, and promises to lead other cities into the future.

Once the boonies, now a hub of innovation, Portland is just beginning to live what's possible. What a wonderful place to call home.

Darcy Winslow is the founder and CEO of DSW Collective.
DSWCollective.com | @DSWCollective

Introduction: This Is "The Portland Bottom Line"

Peter Korchnak

Many tout Portland, Oregon, as an authority on sustainability: progressive urbanism and land-use; alternative transportation; environmental policy; livability. But what about business? How do local companies measure up on sustainability? What cutting-edge sustainable practices have proven to work in Portland's small businesses?

As I delved deeper into my exploration of sustainability and marketing, the questions seemed increasingly pressing. In my search for the best way to explore and publicize the issue, I recalled my experience co-authoring mass-collaboration book projects such as "Connect! Marketing in the Social Media Era" and "Age of Conversation 3: It's Time to Get Busy". Could I employ the same crowdsourcing technique of co-creation to produce a collection of essays highlighting answers to those burning questions?

"The Portland Bottom Line: Practices for Your Small Business from America's Hotbed of Sustainability" is a resounding, "Yes!" I presented the concept at the second "Beyond 2020 Sustainability Unconference", a series of events I coordinated with Renee Spears, one of the book's contributors. As interest grew, it was all a matter of project management and, yes, collaboration. Megan Strand has been a project co-manager par excellence. Without her, the book wouldn't be what it is.

The purpose of "The Portland Bottom Line" is for the city's small businesses to share sustainable practices with their entrepreneurial contemporaries around the United States and abroad. Organized into 12 sections along the triple bottom line of People, Planet, and Prosperity, with each contributor placing their chapter in the desired section, the book explores how small businesses can effectively and efficiently shift toward sustainability and thrive. In their short,

400-word essays, 50 small-business people from the City of Roses share their experiences with sustainability in their companies. "The Portland Bottom Line" demonstrates how small businesses can innovate to put people before profit, help restore the ecosystem, and prosper.

"The Portland Bottom Line" is also a community benefit project. Contributors collectively chose, by vote, the local community organization Mercy Corps Northwest, which supports the launch and growth of sustainable ventures, to receive 100% of profit from the sales of the book.

Enjoy "The Portland Bottom Line"!

Peter Korchnak explores the intersection of marketing and sustainability at Semiosis Communications, and collaborative book creation at GoodBookery.
SemiosisCommunications.com and GoodBookery.com

Megan Strand is a project manager and creative communicator. At InCouraged Communications, she spotlights, connects, and supports businesses that are doing well by doing good.
InCouraged.com | @meganstrand

Part 1: People

The People bottom line gets short shrift in social sustainability: it's hard to define and measure; it's intangible and complex; it's not as sexy as caring for the environment and it's not as immediately profitable. However, people-centered purpose is intrinsic to the best sustainable companies. Whether it's employees, customers, or the community at large, good companies work to empower their people and enrich their social capital.

How has your company benefited humanity with a social purpose? What have you done to motivate and inspire your employees to realize their potential? Why is cultivating deep relationships with your customers central to your business success, and how have you gone about it? How has your business done good in the community and thrived?

In Part 1, Portland's socially-responsible business community reveals the secrets behind its social focus.

1-1 Discover and Manifest Purpose

Social purpose is becoming the mainstay of successful companies. It focuses on benefiting stakeholders, instead of shareholders and takes into account the social context of business. However, taking a compelling "why" at launch and living that purpose in day-to-day operations can be a challenge.

How did you discover your venture's people-driven purpose? In what ways has it served others? How have you communicated from your social purpose? How has your small business put people before profit?

A Meandering Journey Toward True Purpose
Beatrice Benne

The path toward one's life purpose rarely follows a straight line. Linear planning lacks effectiveness in the realms of personal destiny and self-realization. Instead, one must learn to listen to what wants to emerge and remain alert to the signs that impinge upon one's journey. Here is my personal story toward uncovering my co-created purpose.

With a diploma in architecture and my design portfolio under my belt, I moved to the U.S. 15 years ago to find a job. Faced with the difficulties of getting hired, yet motivated by my interest in technology applied to the design process, I returned to school to pursue a Masters, which redirected my career toward information technology. While applying my new skills in the corporate world, I pursued a doctoral degree. Meandering through long years, trying to figure out what my dissertation was truly about, the topic chose me rather than vice versa. The final product, which investigates organizational change from a living systems theory perspective, was the transformational and turning point in my life. My newly emerging purpose was clearly to help both individuals and organizations see themselves as living systems, able to adapt and transform.

I was forced to wait for another two years for the freedom bestowed by a Green Card—the freedom to leave corporate America and move to Portland to pursue—so I thought—my true purpose. In Portland, I co-founded a company with the vision to help local governments look at their sustainability challenges from an adaptive perspective, as opposed to a technical perspective. But after three years, as the original vision evolved with a life of its own—I relearned one does not control much—and despite working with a great team and much opportunity for the future, I heard a familiar voice: "It's time to move on and follow your purpose again."

The fact that the world economy was in a deep recession at the time I resigned did not seem to matter much. Listening is key at those moments. Letting go of fear is fundamental. The message was clear: I had to bring new meaning into my life again. The past nine months have been a new learning journey—a time for reflection, personal development, realignment of the self to my higher Self, finding my voice, and deepening at all levels.

Beatrice Benne is the owner of Soma Integral Consulting, a consulting firm that helps resolve adaptive challenges by transforming and designing purposeful, conscious organizations, while focusing on the well-being of ecosystems.
BeatriceBenne.com | @bcbenne

For the Birds
Amber Turner

Being an environmentalist is for the birds. At least, that's how it started for me. Certainly, people deserve quality of life as well, but I trust birds more as a whole and I plan to reincarnate as a Kingfisher or innocuous Water Ouzel in my next life.

Being a real estate agent in this life, I wondered, how does one take a profession that seems, at first glance, business-suity with assorted paper documents and car travel, and bring in a deeper meaning? I wanted to know why and how the homes I was helping clients buy and sell were hogging so much energy, creating waste and polluting the environment.

The trick is knowing how to make a difference when an opportunity presents itself. I believe it is my duty to try seizing those moments now more than ever. But four years ago I didn't know how to do this. Someone suggested to me that I read building science magazines to learn about green building.

Not my style. Too solitary.

So, I formed a group called GreenPDX and invited others to learn alongside me. Some who joined were already well-versed in green home techniques, while others were as concerned, but naïve, as I was. We're now comprised of 500 members who run the gamut of professions and enthusiasm. Most of all, we're self-motivated learners approaching home tours like sponges, and then spreading what we absorb.

GreenPDX gives us an excuse to invite ourselves into the super-insulated, healthy homes of architects, builders, and green homeowners. The hosts are supportive of the group's endeavor and excited to share their knowledge, and show off their retrofit, recycled residence, or new low-carbon home.

By bringing GreenPDX into my real estate practice, I've become a true believer in that you can make any business sustainable by integrating something you care about and simultaneously educating your clients and peers. Not only do I hope my industry is changing to advocate for healthier homes, I find that more often I get to work with clients whose values mirror my own.

So, while it all started with the birds, I've gained a broader perspective on the importance of a less toxic environment for humans, and I want others to understand how to keep our planet comfortable for centuries to come. And, by reducing our carbon footprint, the water, air, and trees will remain healthy homes for my feathered friends, too.

Amber Turner is a natural match-maker at Living Room Realtors, bringing homes and people together for lasting memories. She is also the founder of GreenPDX, which meets monthly for home tours or guest speaking events.
GreenPDX.com

Regional Art: Buy Local

Janelle Fendall Baglien

I used to think "buy local" meant strawberries. Hoods to be exact. That was back in my farm girl days—we were a fourth generation Oregon farm family. We'd go over to Mrs. Hanuska's and pick a couple of crates of sweet berries and help my Grandpa make jam. Sustainability, buy local, green—it was a way of life for us and is ingrained in my soul.

Thirty years later, I am an urbanite, living in Portland and buying local strawberries at New Season's Market. For all I know, they might be from Mrs. Hanuska's farm.

My "buy local" upbringing is now the mission of my own business. I am a dealer and consultant specializing in placing art created by regional artists in corporate environments—the places where we live, work, gather, and heal.

I knew that given the opportunity, business clients would support local artists the good old-fashioned way: by buying it, if they had an easy way to do so. It was a perfect win-win. Clients get great art, artists make money, and soulless buildings become homes to creations that connect community.

Art was a hard world to break into. People thought I was nuts for trying to make a living from it but with hard work and passion, anything is possible. My farm is now my stable of artists. My crop is now a website full of hundreds of regional artists and thousands of works of art. The result of the harvest can be witnessed in projects like the Hotel Modera in downtown Portland, which features 500 works of art by local painters, photographers, sculptors, and print makers.

The best part of my job is writing checks to artists and seeing a place become saturated with soul through the hand of a local artist.

To get even deeper into the sustainability movement, we now provide art reproductions on paper made of elephant poop (yes, that's right), bamboo, and other FSC-certified materials.

What started as a dream in 2005 is now a thriving business. The concept of "buy local" works for strawberries and it works for art. And it can work for almost any product or service one has a passion to create.

Janelle Fendall Baglien is President of Studio Art Direct, which provides turnkey corporate art programs created by regional artists and which is considered the nation's largest source for art by Portland-area artists.

StudioArtDirect.com

Green Dreaming: A Conscious Evolution

Thaddeus Ruyer

As controversial as it may be to state, the universe started without humans, and it could very well go on without us.

The objective of sustainability is to preserve an earth that is inhabitable for humans and for no other purpose. The vegetation and animal species preservation is also directed to preserve earth for humanity.

There are two universal laws that any lay person can understand and accept and they are:

1. Murphy's Law: "If something can go wrong, it will."
2. Nothing is perfect—perfection does not exist.

These laws are in fact very well fitted to explain humanity and human behavior.

Sustainability is more than just protecting the environment so that we can continue on our journey of conscious evolution, whether we are aware of it or not. Sustainability will, in fact, teach us the universal truth that although many of us have realized but that we are yet to acknowledge.

That Universal Truth is: Until we love each other as one regardless of our apparent different origins on a global scale, there will be no sustainable sustainability.

There is only one earth, one atmosphere, one ecosystem.

As the gradual deterioration accelerates more in one region than in others, masses of people will be migrating to more livable regions, potentially creating conflicts even wars between us.

The only self sustainable energy is the energy of love, as love begets love.

Ultimately there cannot be only pockets of preserved environments, this is not a competition between cultures and regions, this is the next step in human evolution, the day must come in which we are one.

One way to start is with one person at a time, with ourselves and to promote this behavior by example at work, at home and with every person we come in contact with until there is a quantum leap in consciousness and we all are the same.

With this in mind I have applied this principle at work by reinforcing respect and kindness towards my staff and, in case that a correction is needed, I will first find something good to complement the performance of the employee and then after establishing a caring connection. I will then communicate the correction and accomplish my goal.

The energy of love is a self-sustainable energy, ever creating, expanding, and realizing.

Thaddeus Ruyer is architect, real estate broker, developer, human spirituality-consciousness apprentice, artist, sculptor, and musician.

Eating Sustainably

Judith Yamada

Following an early retirement from a career in juvenile justice, I felt drawn to starting a business providing a useful, healthy and sustainable product or service. Investing a few hundred hours and a good deal of money to become a certified aromatherapist, I entered a partnership making organic personal care products. Within two years, the business became an overwhelming burden for my partner, who has small children and a full-time job. In 2008 we closed, and I felt hurt and defeated.

After a few months of healing, I looked for a part time job, with no success. I'd watch the news and the jobless rate and I'd fume. What could be done to bring money into communities and increase employment? What could I do?

Researching options, I discovered the Sustainable Table website. It's educational, empowering and all about food: what we eat, seasonal eating, land use practices, and humane treatment of farm workers and livestock.

Subsequently, with a long unused degree in restaurant management, love of culinary arts, and years of professional cooking and baking, I became a seasonal eater and local consumer. Then I put up my website and began teaching classes at the neighborhood Community Center. Portland Home Cooking was open for service.

I believe in the importance of this mission and sustain my seasonal soapbox by advocating for family farms, teaching seasonal cooking, promoting local shopping, volunteering for Friends of Family Farmers, sharing advice and recipes on my blog and online articles, and developing new seasonal recipes.

Many consumers don't realize that buying oranges from Australia, asparagus from Costa Rica, or grapes from Chile does more than impact the environment. That well-traveled food is stale and less nutritious upon arriving at its destination. This sort of spending has a negative impact on our local food sources, businesses and jobs.

Sadly, more than 300 farmers leave the land every week. If they can't make a living on the farm, our scenario for fresh food in the future is alarming. Buying seasonally helps family farms remain viable. These careful stewards of the land (unlike corporate farms) spend most of their money close to home. The more they can spend, the better. The farmer's spending benefits local business, and positively impacts my community, my neighbors, and me.

Judith Yamada, an advocate for family farms, uses her culinary training and experience to teach seasonal, sustainable food preparation and purchasing.

PortlandHomeCooking.com

Doing Good Is Feeling Good

Jonathan Davis

In 2005, I entered the 'real' world following my family's footsteps in finance. I had no career focus after college and I didn't know what I wanted to associate myself with. So, I went with what was familiar.

I was on the path.

The economy was hot and, unknowingly, I entered it at the beginning of the end. I was on the path to creating roots with my new company and relationships with those in the industry. That was all for naught, because that company shut its doors for good.

In the few years I was in finance I earned chest pains from stress by working with the overly greedy, unprofessional, and unethical. With all that said, I'm thankful for what I learned about the industry.

You've heard it before. Timing is everything.

Knowing that I was going to be laid off, but not knowing when, introspection and reflection heightened self-awareness in what I wanted to associate myself with. I wanted to be a part of something that did good for people, or the planet, or animals...something!

I searched online for a resource in sustainable living for the Portland, Oregon area to find something of interest. I couldn't find what I was imagining, so I thought I'd create it myself. Eight months later, GreenPosting.org was launched as the best resource for sustainable living in the Portland area.

Learning on the fly.

Embarking in a new field of work and community, I had no idea what to expect or how I would be received. I've never been an entrepreneur nor did I have strong relationships in the local green business community. I started by immersing myself to see if I was making a mistake. On top of green networking, I sat down for coffee and sent emails to people who were already established in Portland's green business community for their feedback.

The positive responses about creating GreenPosting and the feeling of open arms by those in the green community was not only surprising, but motivating for me to continue pushing the ball uphill in launching GreenPosting.org and growing it with content, outreach, advertisers, and now consulting.

I don't know what's in store for GreenPosting. However, I do know that sustainability is an area of business that I will continue to associate myself with. I found that doing good is feeling good.

Jonathan Davis is the Founder of GreenPosting.org.
GreenPosting.org | @GreenPosting

1-2 Engage Your Employees

Your company is primarily, not a legal entity or physical space, but a network of people. Your employees are the front line of your small business brand. They keep your company going.

What methods or tools have you used to help your employees succeed? In what ways do your employees have a say in the company and how do you keep them happy? How have you motivated employees to do their best and enjoy their jobs without feeling like their work is drudgery? What benefits has your company realized from happy, healthy employees?

Skipping Along as a Happy Steak Slave

Sharon Soliday

With over-filled plates in hand, medium rare steak juice running down my arms, I'd rub against the back counter to twist my blue-green plaid polyester uniform skirt back into place, eight times a night. A giant plastic slab of flesh-toned meat rose 30 feet in the air outside the front door. My soul was being chipped away in indentured servitude at Happy Steak.

Power was important to my manager at Happy Steak. He spent a great deal of time and resources ensuring we understood he was the boss. At nineteen, I spent an equal amount of effort assuring him I didn't care.

I counted the days until I could quit.

Fast-forward to a professional career of stylish clothes and evenings free of carnivores licking the edges of a T-Bone. I had a door and a phone, and, shockingly, various bosses who spent a great deal of time explaining to me they were the boss.

I counted the days until I could quit.

I vowed my company would be different. I was determined to create a sustainable workforce, people that loved their work and loved the company. This was the workforce I wanted. And by giving up the need to be in charge, I have watched an idea blossom into a company where staff often apologize if life changes must take them away.

My job isn't to know all the answers. My job is to encourage questions. My job is to dream a bigger dream than anyone in the room.

My tip for a sustainable workforce? Turn the power of running your business over to your staff.

Provided some structure, my staff decide their work schedule, how much they want to work, where they will work, and how much they'll make. No, it's not impossible. Ten percent is clear communication, 90% is actually trusting staff. Given the autonomy to make decisions and follow through, most people do.

With practice, courage, and trust we removed further constructs and now have staff identify how they want to be recognized for a job well done, what they want to learn more about, and how we should celebrate company success.

I mean really, what would have been different if Happy Steak Manager had put me in charge for a day?

You know, besides the uniform.

Sharon Soliday is a happy, powerless visionary.
TheHelloFoundation.com

Create a Future Worth Living Into

Susan Bender Phelps

Ever try to predict the future? Notice how often you are right? That's because we predict what we know is already possible. In the 1990s, I led mentoring programs for at-risk youth—12- to 14-year olds certain they would never finish high school and doubtful about whether they would live past 25. The program was based on the premise that the most powerful way of living is to create the future instead of predicting it. Adult mentors worked one-to-one with each student for a year. To recruit the students I would share about a new possibility for the future and how the mentors would help them make positive changes and reach their goals.

A typical recruit, Jordan, a 6th grader in special education, reading at a 1st grade level, getting D's and F's, sent to the principal's office twice a week, oldest of five children with a single mom, and the only one who wasn't medically fragile. He wanted to earn Bs. Based on his past, he could only predict he would continue to do poorly. Yet, when he saw the glimmer of a possibility for a future he could create and the promise of a support system, he had the courage to try.

Improving his reading was the first step. His mentor worked with him, encouraging and supporting him relentlessly. As his reading improved, so did his writing. Within six months, Jordan was mainstreamed and getting B's. To this day, he has a good job, is married with children, and maintains a relationship with his mentor.

What does this have to do with sustainability, employee engagement and the future of your business? It used to be understood that you got an entry level job, worked hard for a promotion, and climbed the career ladder one rung at time. Today, there's no ladder, and when there's no ladder, employees cannot imagine a bright future. It affects their work, loyalty, behavior, and decisions.

We know mentoring transforms kids like Jordan. Every day we are proving it can transform the companies where his generation is employed because effective professional mentoring programs demonstrate to employees that their future is as important as that of the organization. Mentors can see that their knowledge, skills and experience are valued. The whole company is strengthened when you develop the talent within. A strong company is a sustainable company because it is a company with a vibrant future.

Susan Bender Phelps is a professional mentoring and leadership development expert. She speaks about and teaches skills that lead to breakthrough performance and dynamic career growth.

OdysseyMentoring.com | @OdysseyMentor

When Should You Let Your Employees Run the Company?

Robert Zahrowski

I am going to discuss a successful approach used by my clients, such as Pacific Power & Light, PGE, and others, to develop successful solutions to complex business problems, which will also work for you in a small business.

Three critical points to a small business owner's success:

- Realization the owner does not know everything
- A passion for product/service quality
- Value of customers' and employees' desires

First, realize there is a problem. Some typical symptoms are: Your employees are not happy; customers are complaining; you're becoming increasingly involved in decisions that you feel the employees should make; profit margins and sales are down; your company is losing market share; you need to invest in new technology; you have a feeling that things are not going smoothly.

Second, define the actual problem, which is sometimes called root-cause analysis. Ask, "Why is this happening?"

Third, calculate how much you are losing in dollars. This is where everything is converted to dollars. Your calculation will be the most accurate. Convert such things as waste of product and/or material, waste of employee hours (time is money) hours x salary + benefits, production costs per unit, sales reduction, lost customers. What is it worth to you to make the problem go away?

Fourth, choose your most respected and skillful employees to find the solution. The team will know more about the process than you.

Fifth, give the team the following charter of tasks:

1. Identify what is wrong with the current process.
2. Develop a list of solutions that will correct the problem.
3. Recommend the best alternative solution(s).
4. Calculate a budget and time frame for implementation.
5. Submit a cost savings analysis.
6. Outline the implementation of the project, and assure it will not negatively impact any other other processes. (Done while informing others the change is necessary.)
7. Ensure there are no issues created in the new process which are worse than the original problem.

Remember:

1. Your employees are happy you asked them to assist in the future of the company, boosting satisfaction, mutual trust and respect, and morale.
2. The team and you both want success.

This approach gives you a sustainable solution process and improved employee knowledge capital which stays in the company. What could be better?

Robert Zahrowski provides advice on strategic planning, organizational development, process redesign, and productivity improvements to a wide variety of businesses.
RMZahrowski.com

Sustainability Employee Engagement: "Seeing It Through"

Justin Yuen

Today it's much easier to talk about sustainability and employee engagement than it was just a decade ago. Many companies, colleges, government agencies, and nonprofits have made commitments to sustainability at varying levels and typically there are at least a few employees working on sustainability measures.

The challenge now is reaching everyone—not only all employees, but also external stakeholders—and definitively embedding sustainability into culture and decision-making. By effectively engaging everyone your company interacts with you'll achieve greater: acceptance of new company policies; responsibility to implement new behaviors voluntarily; innovation as inspired employees engage in a process of shared discovery.

Having a comprehensive and collaborative effort involving all stakeholders includes:

1. Communicating vision

This step builds context for the significant change required for a sustainable and prosperous future. Many avenues are required to educate everyone so they're on the same page with a definition of sustainability, ideas for 2020 goals, and potential results. Making this scalable and cost-effective while maximizing reach is critical. Suggested resource: The Natural Step Network.

2. Diffusing innovation

Once everyone understands the vision, things shift to the responsibilities of each person and team in figuring out innovative ideas and putting them into practice. To catalyze this, take advantage of tools to empower more and more people to take action at all levels. We're social creatures, so when employees lead, their peers notice and are more likely to follow.

Suggested resource: the Northwest Earth Institute's "Sustainable Systems at Work" program.

3. Building culture

Once businesses have come up with ideas and action plans, there needs to be an ongoing way for everyone involved to update their progress, share best practices, find internal experts to answer questions, track the progress and celebrate your successes. Here's where you can leverage social media platforms with tools for action.

Suggested resource: FMYI's collaboration software.

It will take time for these three components to become fully integrated into daily operations practices, but cost-effective tools are available. This process is effective for sustainability engagement, but is also a framework for innovation in general. At the end of the day, it's about having shared vision, gathering ideas from a broad range of teams, taking action, and providing a way for ongoing learning while measuring progress.

Justin Yuen is President of FMYI, a collaboration software company, and a change agent.
FMYI.com | @FMYI

1-3 Cultivate Customer Relationships

Sustainable businesses satisfy real human needs. Central to accomplishing that is building and maintaining long-term relationships with your customers. Not only is repeat business less expensive, it makes you a part of your customers' lives and a part of their community.

What creative methods or tools have helped you cultivate meaningful relationships with your customers? What methods or actions inspire trust in your customers, and motivate their loyalty? How have you turned your company into a responsible member of the community?

Conversation, Community, and Commerce: The Three C's of Sustainable Business

David Anderson

I learned years ago that 80% of consulting involved putting myself in a customer's situation. By connecting on a personal level, I better understood their problem and could offer a solution that served their needs. The simplest way to accomplish this was to listen. Back then, I hadn't yet heard the phrase "sustainable business", but if I had, I would have understood listening to be a major component of it.

Today, connecting with a customer is more important than ever. Our Web hosting company handles hundreds of support requests each week, and the solution to every problem always begins by understanding things from a customer's perspective. A personal conversation builds a sense of camaraderie, trust, and even friendship. Finding the solution becomes a positive experience for the customer. As a result, we earn their trust and repeat business.

We've developed our understanding of the process into a philosophy called "the Three C's":

- Conversation
- Community
- Commerce

Connection builds conversation. In an age of faceless corporations, customers increasingly and rightfully want to do business with companies they can speak with and know on a personal level. The most successful sales and enduring client relationships always begin by showing someone the human face of our company and striking up an open conversation.

Conversation builds community. Inspired communication builds common ground with others. This can quickly grow into a community of like-minded individuals centered around your business and values. We've built on this notion and actively connect our customers to one another. We're creating a closed loop system of customers that relate to one another in a supportive, sustainable manner.

Community builds commerce. A neighbor would rather ask for a cup of sugar from a neighbor down their street than a complete stranger, and a community would rather do business with itself than choose random suppliers beyond its borders. A community naturally supports its members in a sustainable manner, and in a closed loop community, business is driven from within and gives back to itself.

In the new sustainable economy, people want to do business with companies aligned with their own values. By applying the principles of the Three C's, we have used the art of conversation to connect with our customers on a powerful level, and joined them together to create a supportive and prosperous community. This approach can be applied by any business that cares to learn how. Simply converse with your customers, foster the connections into community, and cultivate trust into sustainable commerce that can last.

David Anderson is Principal of Canvas Dreams, a sustainable Web hosting provider, which uses renewable energy and is a certified B Corporation Web host.
CanvasDreams.com | @canvasdreams

The Cycling Professional

Mike Russell

Awkward: going into a professional event or meeting with a cycling pannier, helmet, and (when the weather demands it) full-body rain gear. Because my bicycle is my primary means of transportation, I have no place to leave my belongings; everything follows me in.

Admittedly, no one has ever derided my cycling or openly questioned my professional qualifications because of my bag and helmet. Perhaps that's because cycling is a ubiquitous part of Portland's culture. Perhaps it's because people keep their thoughts to themselves. Nevertheless, I can't shake the initial anxiety upon arrival.

Conversely, I never tire of the relief and camaraderie I feel when I see someone else's bike gear at the meeting. Such accoutrements make the resounding declaration: "I didn't drive to get here." Regardless of business, it's a pleasure to meet a kindred spirit of the road. Any initial formality evaporates as conversation sparks around riding conditions and drifts into business.

Granted, cycling isn't a possibility for everyone. Our actions and choices must align with our circumstances and resources. But whatever your situation, you can always afford a brief compliment. Such encouragement may reinforce the cyclist's resolve and inspire anyone else nearby to reconsider his own commuting choices.

Despite the allure of great exercise, endless fun, and affirming your convictions, becoming a bike-commuter may seem like an enormous speed bump. Break it down into manageable chunks and don't start in winter. Choose one day during nice weather when you only need to go to one location. Multiple errands are possible with a little forethought; can you plan a route from the post office to the school and then swing by the grocery store on the way home?

(Bonus: This sort of hyper-local living and conscientious planning is readily transferable to the car; you could reduce your driving time—and carbon footprint—dramatically.)

Best of all, look at the extra travel time as an opportunity to catch your breath, reflect on your day, and observe your town from a fresh perspective. Being indoors all day may not seem so bad when you have a nice ride home waiting for you.

Be safe. Be informed. Visit the Bicycle Transportation Alliance website at BTA4Bikes.org, or your local bike store first. They'll be happy to meet a burgeoning spirit of the road.

Mike Russell defends the reader's intelligence, champions his client's message, and conspires to promote the sustainability movement.

PivotalWriting.com

Building Relationships By Making A Difference

Tom Dwyer

Tom Dwyer Automotive Services is an independent automotive repair shop tucked away in the historic Sellwood neighborhood. Like Portland itself, the shop is comfortable and laid-back with friendly people, wi-fi, books, and great coffee.

Even in a city known for its leftward bend, I think our business stands out. Over a 30-year history the shop has built a reputation for quality, integrity, environmental consciousness, community involvement, and sustainability. Our long-time presence on Portland's only progressive talk radio station helped us become a Portland icon.

But, like all businesses, Dwyer's has to attract new clients on a continuing basis to thrive. Knowing how most of my clients felt about the environment and sustainability, I thought that might be a good starting point. But rather than just telling people how eco-conscious the shop already was, I decided to create a new project that would let the clients actually participate.

We met with Bonneville Environmental Foundation, which sells offsets for carbon consumption. Together we built a membership program, in which Bonneville would provide offsets for vehicle use, and our shop would provide coupons worth $350 toward services ($350 to link with 350.org). The program would strengthen relationships with existing clients, be a strong inducement for potential clients, reinforce the shop's green credentials, and return the client many times their cost of investment.

That was 2007. In its first year, the Tom Dwyer Automotive Carbon Neutral Program ("CNP") removed over 700,000 pounds of carbon from the air. As of July 2010, the total stands at 1,430,400 pounds, enough to power 82 homes a year.

We hoped to make a difference when we started, but this is a much bigger difference happening much sooner than we expected. The carbon offsets are essentially free to people who sign up for CNP because of all the discounts we provide to members. Since we promote CNP in our marketing, an expanding group of people is constantly exposed to the idea of carbon neutrality. We benefit because the people who care are the kind of people who appreciate our company and the service we provide. It's been a win-win all around, and we think it's exactly the kind of sustainable model businesses in the future will need to survive.

Tom Dwyer is the owner of Dwyer Automotive Services, Inc.
TomDwyer.com

Set Yourself Apart in Your Professional Service Business

Glenn Maynard

Service business owners are typically devoted to their professional development and spend a lifetime perfecting technical skills. Mastery of a craft is an essential pillar of building a loyal clientèle, but providing an exceptional experience for your customers involves more than proficiency.

When you attract clients who are compatible with your approach, it saves you marketing dollars because they refer other clients to you. Clients who realize you're providing information and philosophies that are new and exciting to them also tend to show appreciation by referring, because you have provided an unexpected value. Our business has found the following factors have given us an added advantage in attracting like-minded clients:

1. Appealing physical space
2. Educational philosophy
3. State of the art training
4. Impeccable service
5. Client-oriented programming

Working in a beautiful physical space with plenty of light, air, and a view of trees provides an uplifting environment to staff and visitors. Colorful, unique furnishings and attractive artwork establish a lively atmosphere. Clients enter a waiting room with quality reading materials, useful books and brochures, and educational games and audios.

Our staff members regard our clients as fellow learners. We have resources and tools we share with clients, but we are not the experts on their lives. Counseling and therapy services cannot be effective if they ignore the social context in which problems occur. Families affected by the economy; individuals facing unemployment because of corporate instability; young people who are worried about the environmental degradation they will grapple with in the future; all benefit from an opportunity to make sense of misfortune and tragic events by seeing the bigger picture.

We keep our training up-to-date and investigate ever-evolving innovative methods to provide personalized solutions. Holding onto tradition for the sake of tradition is unsustainable, and as our research and learning progresses, we share that with our clients.

We model healthy and reasonable lifestyle choices and practice the same good self-care that we promote for our clients: getting exercise, enjoying nature, and investing our time and energy locally. This allows us to provide a high quality of service because we arrive refreshed and ready to be dynamic and engaging.

Clients get support for being finished with counseling or coaching services as soon as they're ready to be. We want them to become the most capable people possible, equipping them with the tools, knowledge, strategies, and confidence they seek.

Glenn Maynard, LPC, has extensive experience in administrative finance. He owns Portland Coaching and Counseling Center and specializes in addiction recovery.
PortlandCoachingandCounseling.com | @PDX_Counseling

Building Relationships by Giving Back

Jennifer Forti

The mission of *the people's republic of portland* ("*prop*") is to celebrate everything that makes Portland unique by promoting local businesses who share in the same values. This philosophy resonates well with people creating a very positive response, which helps to build and foster wonderful relationships with my customers and the public. They know I have the community's best interests in mind.

I believe in the power of face-to-face connections, a speedy follow-through and in-person delivery. When a customer places an order, we make sure that it's delivered in a timely fashion, ideally by bike (weather-permitting, of course).

Acquainting ourselves with the owners and managers is essential to *the people's republic of portland* as it allows for a personal connection, which is something that goes a long way when building a business relationship. Cross promotion and collaboration with the business owners by finding creative ways to help each other thrive is especially valuable in times of economic instability.

I always make sure my customers know I have a fan page on Facebook and a presence on Twitter that we can use for mutual promotion of our businesses.

In addition, we are striving to become a B, or Beneficial, Corporation, which involves implementing business policies that show the company as one of transparency, dedicated to making people, planet, and profit benefit without compromising one or the other. This is tremendously important to our organization as it makes us feel part of a larger, socially and environmentally responsible community.

More than just selling t-shirts, *prop* stands for a brand with a conscience and a message: Community makes all the difference. Because this is something we advocate for, we will be giving back to four local non-profits at the end of the year.

There's nothing like the feeling of doing good: It leaves you with a sense of accomplishment and empowerment, ultimately benefiting everyone.

Jennifer Forti is the founder of the people's republic of portland.
thepeoplesrepublicofportland.com | *@theprop*

1-4 Benefit the Community

In addition to employees and customers, the community also benefits from your company's social purpose. Supporting causes, devoting time and resources, even shifting your business model toward the greater good can create tremendous positive impact. You can do well by doing good.

How has your small business fit into the context of your community? What avenues of doing well by doing good have you explored and what benefits have you received as a result? How have you used your company's resources to benefit the community?

My Best Day at Work
Renee Spears

Recently someone in my office said, "Today is my best day at work ever." My mind flashed back to my best day at work. Most people probably think it would be the day when our company won the Small Business of the Year Award or was named the #1 Company to Work For, but it wasn't.

My best day started out as any other day. I came to work in my shorts and flip flops and was greeted by Stella, a co-worker's dog. After having a cup of tea and saying good morning to everyone, I settled down to work.

It happened to be Earth Day that day. Everyone at work either rode their bikes, took public transportation or carpooled to the office in an effort to conserve. We also celebrated with a lunch feast from Burgerville. After gorging ourselves on spicy black bean burgers and strawberry shakes, I checked to see which loans had closed that day and was told that we'd closed 4 deals for first-time home buyers. It's great fun when we get to share in the excitement of someone buying a first home. This in itself was a great day, but the part that made it the best happened after lunch.

Years earlier I had started a donation program where we give $100 to our client's choice of non-profit each time we close a loan. For the past 5 years, I'd been writing checks to non-profits. Our client's choices range from the Rock and Roll Camp for Girls to the Oregon Food Bank and everything in between. That day I wrote a check to Raphael House of Portland for $500.

It didn't hit me what had just happened until I went out to record this transaction with the rest of our donations on the office bulletin board and did some math. That day, the total of our donations topped $100,000. Amazing! Only 5 years earlier I'd started the business in my family room and now we'd given back $100,000 to the community. It was actually possible to make a difference in the world! I'd never felt pride like I did that day!

That was my best day at work ever.

Renee Spears is President of Rose City Mortgage, the nation's 1st socially responsible mortgage company, named by Oregon Business Magazine the state's #1 Small and #4 Green Company.
RoseCityMtg.com | @RoseCityMrtg

Put People Ahead of Profits

Perry Gruber

Greyston Bakery and Zappos.com both illustrate this counterintuitive but potent strategy.

You've probably heard of Zappos. Greyston is more interesting. Started by a Zen master / aerospace engineer / entrepreneur in 1982, Greyston didn't start out to become the exclusive brownie producer for Ben & Jerry's. Nor did it plan to churn out 20,000 pounds of ice cream mix-ins daily. That engineer-turned-Zen-master wanted to give jobs, healthcare, housing and education to underprivileged people. *USA Today*, the *Oprah Show*, *New York Magazine* and other major media outlets have featured them. How did they grow so successful? By putting people ahead of profits. What does that look like?

- Create a cause brand: Wrap your brand in a story that you personally believe in, something that makes the world better.
- Implement your cause from the beginning. Don't wait until you're profitable.
- Strive to constantly make the story better and better. Stay ahead of copycats by constantly iterating your story.

It's more than cause marketing or corporate social responsibility or even being sustainable. In fact, chuck the buzz words. This is about making your business human. Humans care. So can your business. Customers like businesses that care:

1. 92% of people have a more positive image of a company that supports a cause they care about.
2. 87% are likely to switch from one product to another—price and quality being equal—if the other product is associated with a good cause.*

You can still make money the traditional way. You may create the next iPad or Google, or Snuggie. But, is that likely? Maybe. Even so, relate your business story to a cause. Tell that story and you'll be ahead, especially in markets where competitors aren't doing this.

My company, NedWater, is not Greyston or Zappos, but the story is similar. Substantial portions of gross revenues support non-profits; we work strategically with non-profits in ways that create passive revenue for them. NedWater customers get in on the giving, allowing their businesses to benefit from good-deed blowback. Our product is substantially delivered by bike and our focus is always local. Our success isn't certain. No startup's is. But the trend is with us. By putting the planet and people ahead of profits, NedWater may be ahead of the trend.

* Source: 2007 Cone Consumers Research Survey

Perry Gruber is Co-founder / CEO of NedWater, the world's first cause-driven drinking water company.
NedWater.net | @ned_perry

How to Make a Solo Business Sustainable in Portland Regardless of the Economy

Kaya Singer

Portland is brimming with free-willed individuals with entrepreneurial spirit, who, in following their passion, decided to begin a small business.

Whether people are health practitioners, coaches or designers, Portland solo-business owners are often motivated by wanting to make a difference in their community via their business.

This special category of entrepreneurs seem to abound in Portland. People feel called to offer a service that is purposeful, and, at the same time, that helps their clients and customers to be happier, healthier, and more sustainable in themselves.

There are two major challenges that many small solo-business owners have to face right at the get go. Number one, they usually begin with a cash shortage, and therefore not enough money to invest in their business. In simple terms, they are facing personal sustainability challenges, which causes stress and a need to bring money into their business quickly.

Second, they tend to focus entirely on their service as this is their skill and expertise. One woman I know identifies as an acupuncturist first and as an entrepreneur second. In fact, she is a great practitioner but a poor business owner. She lacks solid business skills and she often struggles to create the cash flow she needs to survive. Like her, many solo-business owners have no marketing or business plan and they suffer from self-doubt. As a result they compare themselves to others and feel afraid to take risks.

So what we see is talented and large group of small business owners who care deeply about their community and want to make a difference, but whose energy is entirely focused on getting more clients. They are lacking in the sustainability they need to be able to give more on a broader level. Some people blame it on the economy, but in fact it is all about focusing on what can be controlled. This includes:

1. Developing a marketing plan based on a strong niche
2. Creating a business plan strategy from that place
3. Overcoming self-doubt
4. Getting help

Sustainability needs to begin with the business owner and then it will trickle down to their team and to their customers.

I tell people, "Don't worry about the world economy, pay attention to your own business and look at what you can do right now." Small business owners have the ability to make a huge impact in the greater community, but that won't happen until they become sustainable in themselves first.

Kaya Singer is the owner of Awakening Business Solutions and the author of "Clear Your Focus Grow Your Business".
AwakeningBusiness.com | @kayasinger

Progressing from 'Pro Bono' to 'Paid'

Jennie Vinson

I decided to start my business in December 2008. Like many people at the end of 2008, I was a victim of the financial crisis and had been laid off from my job. Facing an uphill job-search battle, I decided to give it a go on my own. I knew that the chances of getting a job in a market where companies all over town were unloading their marketing departments was going to be slim. So after a two-hour conversation with a trusted mentor, I came home and told my husband that I was going to start my own business.

As a marketing business, the good news is that you don't need much capital to get started. I bought a new laptop, increased the minutes on my cell phone and had a designer friend of mine create some business cards. Then I set out to find my first client.

Soon the self-doubt crept in: How would I find this client? Whom would I target? How much would I need to spend to acquire these clients? I decided that my company's marketing strategy would be to give my time, energy, and services away to organizations I was passionate about. I wasn't sure this was going to lead to new, paying clients, but it would be a way for me to get out there and learn what I could.

I worked pro bono for both non-profit organizations and small businesses I felt were making a contribution to the community. Here's what I learned:

1. Each one of the pro-bono clients I worked with naturally referred me to other businesses and organizations. This wasn't my intention when I started, nor did I request these referrals. But doing good work for my community resulted in new clients for my business.

2. The experience that I gained working in a variety of dynamic organizations built a foundation of expertise, from which I could reach out to potential paying clients.

3. Doing work for my community has become a natural extension of my business model. It inspires other creative talent to work with me and my paying clients feel a greater loyalty to my organization because of this commitment.

It is important to stay in integrity about how your business utilizes pro-bono work to benefit your business. It can be a slippery slope into greenwashing, pinkwashing, etc.

Jennie Vinson is the owner of Mission First Marketing, a native Oregonian, and a creative marketing strategist working with mission-driven businesses in Portland and beyond.

MissionFirstMarketing.com | @missionfirst

Products With a Mission

Doug and MacKenzie Freeman

Mission statements. Many times, they do nothing more than reflect the good intentions of entrepreneurial visionaries. But when we started our media production company with a partner video firm, we looked to our mission statement as a purpose for each educational video we would create and sell.

Our mission statement? "Self-fund the production and marketing of educational videos on sustainability in business that also provide local economic development." In other words, we would showcase the achievements of local, Oregon-based sustainable businesses and their leaders' knowledge so they could serve as international models of green innovation. Their stories would educate business people, and the side-benefit of visibility provided by appearing in our videos might aid in their success.

In support of this mission, we produced three videos on sustainable business. Over several years, these DVDs sold to thousands of entrepreneurs, universities and libraries in 17 countries. So we accomplished the first half of our mission statement: producing and marketing the educational videos.

The part of our mission that required benefiting the community seemed simple enough. Over time, anecdotal evidence revealed that the local business leaders received inquiries about their practices, invitations to speak at events, references in reviews and collateral associated with film festivals that featured the videos, and news coverage due to our marketing efforts. Many participants expressed their appreciation for the benefits they gained.

In retrospect, we should have built in better measures to assess the local economic development impact of the international exposure for participating businesses. Quantitative evidence of a positive return on participation would have helped establish a model that could be duplicated by others to promote sustainable business practices even beyond what we could do as a small company.

The lesson? A mission statement can have value if developed with practical application in mind. Is your mission statement reflected in every product and service you offer? Can you devise ways to ensure that there is some level of local economic development from your work besides that which results directly from your success? And can you set up some types of measurement to assess the positive impact of your endeavor besides income generation for your company?

As you contemplate lofty green mission thoughts, consider how that mission will be integrated with whatever you sell.

Doug and MacKenzie Freeman are Co-owners of Ideascape and Arnold Creek Productions, a sustainability media production company, whose educational videos have won awards, including a Portland BEST, and been shown at film festivals around the world. ArnoldCreekProductions.com

What You Give Defines You

Noland Hoshino

The title of this chapter is a model worth practicing, both personally and in business. Your value and significance isn't what you have, but what you give that develops a lasting impression.

The fancy car, the designer clothes, and having the latest tech gadgets are forgettable after a few days. What's memorable are unselfish acts and giving practices that define your character; donating those designer clothes to a homeless shelter or using that fancy car to deliver meals to the elderly and sick. As a small business owner, I wanted to ensure that our company incorporated a sustainable giving model that reflected our beliefs in engaging and motivating businesses for the greater good.

In a growing market, small businesses must differentiate themselves in order to remain present, relevant and above the fray. It can be done externally or internally with services or products that are unique from the competition. We do it with a payment model that donates to charities or encourages community volunteering, which aligns with our motivation and passion to help others in need.

We donate 5% of our service fees to a client's chosen charity or nonprofit organization. Often, this is the first time the client has made a charitable contribution. It opens the door to further discussion of giving back and building long-term sustainable relationships in the community. It also provides the business another incentive to succeed so that they can continue to make contributions and become something greater than a brick-and-mortar or services business.

We encourage volunteerism with a Service Rewards Program. For every hour that the business volunteers in the community, while under contract, we donate $10 to their chosen charity or nonprofit organization (some rules apply). As the saying goes, "If not us, who?" We want businesses to take action to help others immediately. Studies have shown that corporate volunteer programs have a strong impact in the community with 66% increased partnerships. The benefits are too many and too valuable to ignore.

So, who are you? What do your customers think of you and your business? Think of it this way: At the end of day, what do you want the people to say: "We are gathered here today to remember … had a fancy car and cherished it", or "… gave his time to transport cancer patients to and from chemotherapy in that fancy car he cherished. It was the ride of their life"?

Noland Hoshino is Givologist, Cause Enthusiast, and Chief Social Media Strategist at [B]cause Media Social Media Communciations. BCauseMedia.com | @NolandHoshino

Part 2: Planet

Environmental sustainability should come easiest. Of the three bottom lines, Planet is the most explored, applied, and publicized. It's thanks to "going green" that sustainability has entered the mainstream. But putting a recycling bin in the copy room or turning off the lights is just the beginning.

How have you measured and publicized your achievements in making your business more environmentally sustainable? What else have you done to green up after picking the low-hanging fruit? How have you designed your products, services, processes, or operations to Reduce—Reuse—Recycle?

In Part 2, members of Portland's small-business community share their experiences of delving deeper into environmental sustainability.

2-5 Measure and Report Impact

Making your business more eco-friendly is one thing, demonstrating impact is another. Environmental claims require substantiation and documentation. Measurement, analysis, and reporting are the foundation of your Planet bottom line.

How have you measured your environmental efforts? What reporting methods or frameworks have you used? With whom and how have you shared your measurable outcomes?

How We Measure and Report Impact
Brian C. Setzler, MBA, CPA

We are Certified Public Accountants and operate TriLibrium with triple bottom line values: People, Planet, Profit. Every business needs systems to account for and report on financial performance. Organizations driven by the values of sustainability must also develop systems to account for and report on their social and ecological performance.

Management guru, Dr. Peter F. Drucker, is famous for saying, "You can only manage what you can measure," and, "What's measured improves." Given our goal to operate a socially responsible business with a small environmental footprint, measuring and reporting results is vital to this effort.

There are more than a dozen frameworks to measure and report on an organization's sustainability performance: AccountAbility 1000, Equator Principles, ISO14001, B-Corporation, FSC Certification, and EPA Climate Leaders are just some of the measurement and reporting frameworks an organization could use.

Our firm chose the Global Reporting Initiative ("GRI") framework to benchmark and drive sustainability performance. We consider this the gold standard because of its thoroughness, near-universal applicability and acceptance, and combination of triple bottom line performance into a single report.

Developed through a consensus process from the United Nations Environment Programme, GRI helps an organization develop and create a focused sustainability report. The GRI report is an annual publication that supplements an organization's annual financial report.

An initial GRI report focuses on current year accomplishments and next year's goals across a wide spectrum of GRI indicators which include social, economic and environmental results. Subsequent reports list goals from the previous year's report alongside current year accomplishments before listing next year's goals. This cycle is repeated each year—previous year goals compared to actual accomplishments along with future goals for the coming year.

This report and process provides the transparency increasingly required by the sustainability community and a road map to continuously improved performance.

The end result of this process was a written sustainability report issued in September 2009, which is available electronically on our website. To disseminate this information, we sent all current stakeholders a link to the report. We also refer potential clients, employees, vendors, and others to this information.

We believe our GRI report demonstrates our deep commitment to the values of sustainability and provides a roadmap for where we have been and where we are going. With design and copywriting assistance included, we spent approximately $5,000 to produce our report.

Brian C. Setzler, MBA, CPA, is Founder and CEO at TriLibrium, a certified B-Corp public accounting firm, and a lecturer at the Bainbridge Graduate Institute.
TriLibrium.com | @GreenCPA

A Report Can Do More Than Report

Betsy Henning

"We are AHA!, and we help companies tell their sustainability stories."

I love that sentence. It's bold, honest and positive—qualities at the heart of our business. It's the first sentence of our company's first sustainability report, and the words all but leapt onto the page.

That was the easy part.

It's easy to write about who we are and what we do. We're a communications agency, after all. But documenting what we're doing to be a more sustainable business is more complicated, even for a small (about 35 employees in 2009), private (no shareholders to report to), service-oriented (no supply chain or products) business like ours.

When we set out to create our first sustainability report, we wanted to make it count. We didn't want to pour time and effort into a document that a few people skim and then set aside. We challenged ourselves to do more.

We believe the information companies compile in sustainability reports has potential well beyond the reporting function. It's a reflection of a company's culture and values. It demonstrates smart business strategies. It offers concrete examples of a business's commitment to employees, customers, its community and the environment. In other words, it's a marketing goldmine.

But to be an effective marketing tool, the report needs to be read. We set out to create an engaging report that would serve multiple purposes:

- Document our sustainability efforts and progress.
- Offer big-picture context to our small-business accomplishments.
- Showcase the kind of creative communications work we do for our clients.
- Tell a story about who we are and where we're going.

The result is a narrative with a dynamic design that guides readers through the story, and with interactive elements to delight and inform them along the way.

We publicized it. We promoted it on our blog, website, Facebook and Twitter; we sent out a press release; and we shared it with all of our contacts. The response from clients, employees and members of the CSR community has been incredible.

Our efforts to make our report engaging and accessible paid off. People who knew us learned more about us and our capabilities. And people who may never have heard of us got a bold, honest and positive introduction to AHA!.

Betsy Henning is Principal of AHA!, a strategic communications firm with expertise in writing.
AHA-writers.com | @AHAwriters

Working Towards Zero Waste

Lindsey Newkirk

Elysium Events manages zero-waste programs for events. Through waste reduction, recycling, composting, and donations, zero waste can be used as a goal and a mindset for decision-making.

Challenge

Portland businesses are required to recycle 50% of their waste (75% by 2015). Many of the large public events in Portland have recovery rates less than 30%.

Case Study: The Bite of Oregon

In 2006, the Bite of Oregon event generated 44,000 lbs of material, only 24% (10,560 lbs) of which was recycled. A waste audit found that 55% of the materials thrown in the trash could have been composted.

Over the next two years we worked on a zero-waste program, which resulted in an increase of the recovery rate to 66%. Here's how we did it:

- We created a policy for the 80 vendors to use compostable service ware and to eliminate the use of non-recyclable and non-compostable items.
- We provided composting bins for the public.
- We use management and volunteers to educate the public and sort through materials to remove contaminants.

The Result

The Bite was one of Portland's first successful large-scale public event composting programs.

Metrics

We coordinated with the hauler to obtain separate weights for all of the material that was collected on site. The results were:

1. 45,840 lbs of material generated
2. 30,220 lbs of that was recycled and composted
3. 15,620 lbs went to the landfill

To calculate the recovery rate we used this formula:
(recycling+composting) / (recycling+composting+landfill) x 100
So, 30,220 / 45,840 = 0.66 x 100 = 66% recovery rate

It is also important to calculate waste generated per person. Since attendance numbers vary each year, this metric is a constant baseline in which to compare efforts over time regardless of this variable. Here is the example from the Bite of Oregon:

2006: 55,000 attendees and 33,440 lbs of landfill material: 33,440 / 55,000 = 0.61 lbs of landfill material/person

2008: 45,000 attendees and 15,620 lbs of waste material: 15,620 / 45,000 = 0.35 lbs of landfill material/person

It is important to obtain and track the data in order to evaluate the results of your efforts. Results for zero-waste planning can vary quite a bit depending on the event's strategies and understanding of complexities. It is important to see where you stand, evaluate your program for continued improvements, and report on your efforts. Understanding your results also helps to avoid greenwashing: The truth is in the numbers.

Lindsey Newkirk is the owner of Elysium Events, an event greening company that focuses on zero waste. She has helped her clients reach recovery rates of 66-98%.
ElysiumEventsLLC.com

2-6 Venture Beyond Green Teams

You reduce, reuse, and recycle. You compost. You encourage alternative transportation. You've gone as paperless as humanly possible. Your company's Green Team has picked all the low-hanging fruit.

What's next on your company's eco agenda? What else have you done to make your business more environmentally sustainable? How have you greened the world around your company?

Commuting to Work: It's About the Journey AND the Destination

Caleb Bushner

Myriad studies have demonstrated that a healthy, active employee is a happy, productive employee. After many years of bike and transit commuting I suppose I can attest to this as well as anyone. Portland and its employers have done a great job of removing many of the most prominent barriers to participation on this count: ample, abundant bike lanes and prompt, plentiful bus and light rail options make it possible for a busy professional to get nearly anywhere in the city without ever having to start up his automobile.

As a means of celebrating bike commuting, every September Portland offers a great, competitive, yet friendly, month-long Bike Commute Challenge that, in 2009, had over 11,000 bike commuters log over 1.2 million miles. Portland's employers offer all sorts of incentives to help promote this sort of behavior, but it doesn't just stop at the end of September: Many employers made it easy to bike commute year round by installing showers and gear lockers, not to mention secure, covered storage space for our precious pedal-powered people pushers.

Local government offices produce a specialized water- and tear-resistant map that lists the safest and most preferable routes for tooling around town, specifying low-traffic streets, even pointing out bike shops along the way. As a fun side-effect of all this, the cycling community keeps very close and friendly. I've yet to generate a business lead from a bicycle conversation but two days ago I managed to recruit another member for my weekly pub quiz team!

Portland also produces tools that encourage mass transit use. Developers have created a comprehensive and open-source data package with information about every bus and rail stop in the region. Indeed, this information can now be rendered in augmented reality, meaning that I can point my smartphone in any direction and see a layer of digital bus route information placed over a view of whatever street I'm looking at. I don't have to wait for ages, wondering when the bus will arrive—I can point my phone at the stop I want, learn when the bus is coming and go right back to working until the moment before the bus is set to arrive. My work day is more efficient, prompt, and relaxing for all of these innovations.

Caleb Bushner is a strategy and marketing change agent at From The Rooftops, a Portland-based brand strategy firm. He is also an unrepentant athlete and nerd.

FromTheRooftops.us | @calebbushner

Driving Change: Social Responsibility Is About Differentiation and Innovation

Mitch Rofsky

Business is about innovation, and social responsibility provides real opportunities to be innovative.

Better World Club is a case in point. Most everyone is familiar with auto clubs, roadside assistance, and the 50 million-member AAA. But few consider the roles played by these clubs.

First, as lobbyists. Many Americans recognize the impact of corporate arm twisting, but don't take it into consideration when making purchases. Or maybe they believe that all businesses in an industry (like roadside assistance) are the same.

I founded Better World Club ("BWC") after environmental advocates approached me, looking to take on AAA and the highway lobby. In that effort, BWC, like many innovative businesses, has taken an existing business model and adjusted it to meet social and environmental goals.

BWC exists as a comparable service alternative to other auto clubs and opposes them on a variety of issues from bike lanes to regulating the greenhouse gas emissions of automobiles.

Just as important, though, is that auto clubs are about transportation, an activity responsible for a significant environmental footprint. And that footprint can be significantly reduced through innovation.

To that extent, BWC is in the innovation business. We provide roadside assistance, sure, but we've also pioneered roadside assistance for bicycles, travel carbon offsets, free carbon offsets for auto insurance clients, discounts for alternative fuel vehicle owners, even membership fee discounts for mass transit pass holders. Soon we'll be announcing an effort to persuade our service providers to become greener as well.

In essence, we work to balance the current transportation needs of our customers with their social and environmental values, which requires recognizing and addressing the external costs of transportation and travel (and, of course, minimizing them).

We don't think our efforts come at the expense of the bottom line, either. Rather, we believe that businesses can use social responsibility to differentiate themselves and prosper.

There's another business reason for socially responsible pioneering as well: if you're successful, you're going to be copied. Which means your innovations are going to reach more people.

Better World Club innovated travel carbon offsets and bicycle roadside assistance. AAA Oregon-Idaho copied us. Now, AAA hasn't copied us nationally, which means that they haven't copied us effectively. But, if you're successful, you're going to be copied. And in a way, that's OK. We want more people to have access to our innovations (although we'd like our competition to acknowledge when they copy us).

It just keeps the pressure on to innovate. In business, the pressure to innovate isn't new: It's one of the joys of being in business.

Mitch Rofsky is President of Better World Club.
BetterWorldClub.com

Aluminum Recycling at a Hair Salon
Tess McBride

Most people don't think about the life cycle of the aluminum foil they consume. It emerges from the grocery store, packaged and ready for use like the frozen chicken being unpacked from—hopefully reusable—grocery bags. Even while working at Visual F/X Salon in Northwest Portland, there was little I knew about the foil coming in and out of our business. It arrived in boxed sheets along with hairbrushes and rubber gloves, and was ripped into sections before taking the short trip to a stylist's station and being applied to a client's hair, turning back time by transforming gray hairs into blonds. This common coloring process, known as highlighting, generally requires between 50-75 foils per head, per process. Needless to say, our foil waste added up quickly.

Conservation has always played an important role in our company's business practices. We recycle all that we can: Even our hair clippings are donated to Matter of Trust, an organization that makes hair mats used to soak up oil spills. Consuming such a significant amount of foil contributed to our massive garbage production, requiring a weekly pick up of a large and very full dumpster. As other green businesses can imagine, we felt horrible knowing the amount of waste we were inflicting on the environment. Using less foil sheets wasn't an option, since they're necessary for the quality of service we offer, but we knew there had to be a better option.

We concluded that while we can't reduce the amount of foil we consume, we could reduce our carbon footprint. By discovering a creative way to recycle our used foils, tainted with bleach and peroxide, we've significantly reduced our weekly waste. Creating metal from recycled aluminum foil reduces water pollution by 97 percent, compared to processes of producing new metal. In addition, recycling 1 ton of aluminum saves enough energy to power ten typical households for a year. Our salon donates around 50 large garbage bags of foil annually.

While we can't see providing 10 years of energy, we can see our weekly garbage easily fitting into a family size can. The life cycle we choose for our foil ultimately relates to the life cycle we decide to live and help provide for the future. Practicing green business is a cycle we're happy to support.

Tess McBride is the Communication and Media Outreach Coordinator for Visual F/X Salon, a graduate student at PSU, a recycling nut, and a nature lover.
VisualFXSalon.com | @visualfxsalon

2-7 Design for the Planet

Whether it's physical goods or intangible services, they result from design and require energy and materials. Designing products, services, and processes for minimum environmental impact requires forethought, planning, and creativity. Both environmental sustainability and design start with the right intent.

How have you put design to use for environmental good? How have you incorporated the Reduce – Reuse – Recycle hierarchy into your business? What have you done to continuously innovate in designing for the Planet bottom line?

Getting Involved Leads to Greater Gains

Lisa Holmes

As a graphic designer living in the Midwest, I saw little focus on sustainability around me. I had to stack all of my recyclables in the garage, then load them in my car and schlock them to the recycle center, which was about 12 miles away. We wanted to eat local foods, but couldn't find them in the local stores, so we grew them in a home garden, canning and freezing produce for use throughout the year.

Moving to Portland was an easy choice. Moving my business was a harder one, but with Portland's focus on sustainability, I knew it would give me a chance to work with companies with that focus.

After moving here, to get to know the Portland design community, I joined the board of AIGA Portland as Secretary. While this AIGA chapter had held several sustainability-related events, there wasn't a focus on sustainability covering everything it did. I wanted to know what kind of impact a designer can have regarding sustainability and wanted to help protect Oregon's incredible natural environment. So I worked to create a new Sustainability Chair board position. Then I spent a year working on a mission, goals, and forming a green team of designers to help me work on this initiative. Since then, we have:

- created online resources with a focus on local vendors that provide sustainable design-related products and services;
- begun a quarterly event series: "SHIFT: A Green Salon" with 10 presenters giving 5-minute presentations on what sustainable design means to them; and
- started holding quarterly "Green Salon Meetups" where designers get together to discuss sustainable design in an informal setting.

To provide exposure for the local sustainable design vendor community, we held "ReSource: Green Design Expo" on Earth Day 2010 with a vendor trade show, mini-seminars given by the vendors, and a program of speakers discussing market research and consumer brands with a focus on sustainability.

Since beginning the sustainability initiative at AIGA Portland, I have gained so much through my collaboration with other like-minded sustainability geeks. I've learned how designers can and do make a difference. This knowledge has helped me gain work with great clients who are doing good in the world. And, this effort has enabled other small business owners get up to speed on sustainability.

Lisa Holmes is a principal at Yulan Studio, a design firm specializing in web, interactive, and print.
YulanStudio.com | @LisaDHolmes

The SOL Principles

Aaron Harmon

We joke that our company name is a triple-entendre: "Sol" is Spanish for "sun", an homage to the paleta and our Latin American culinary heritage, and it also sounds like "soul". Making our customers happy is good for our souls.

"SOL" is also an acronym for "Sustainable—Organic—Local". We call them the SOL Principles, and they are our company's Vision Statement. We reflect upon them with every decision as we grow and evolve. Sometimes we pay a higher price because of the SOL Principles, but often find the more ethical choice is less expensive than the alternative.

Ingredients. High quality, ethically-sourced ingredients are central to our business model. We use local organic ingredients wherever possible to reduce the aggregate number of "food miles traveled" for our pops. If it isn't local, we buy Certified Organic. We also look beyond "organic" to consider fair labor practices, carbon footprints, recyclability, etc. We encourage consumers to look beyond certifications to see what they are really getting.

Bags. Our bags are "Grade 4 polypropylene", recyclable with plastic grocery bags. We are testing a water-soluble film that is compostable in residential bins. If it withstands freezer testing, our packaging will then be 100% compostable.

Sticks. Our sticks are made of white birch, a rapidly renewable tree species, and are certified by the Forest Stewardship Council. We are the only frozen novelty company in the world registered with the Forest Stewardship Council ("FSC").

Boxes. Our boxes are 100% post-consumer recycled content, certified by both FSC and Sustainable Forestry Initiative ("SFI").

Carbon footprint. We vend from 1970s-era cooler tricycles. To minimize our carbon footprint, we pedal to farmers markets whenever feasible. Since Portland is so bike-friendly, our trikes are a hit with kids both big and small.

Composting and recycling. We compost 100% of our organic waste, and have a sophisticated recycling program.

Community outreach. To divert popsicle sticks from the waste stream, we established a recycling program where we wash and bleach them for crafts.

Vegan-friendliness. Our pops are vegan and gluten-free. We use coconut for our cream pops because of the petroleum and fertilizers required to grow corn for cow feed. It's also an animal cruelty issue, since many dairy animals are treated poorly in organic and conventional facilities. Also, the unfortunate byproduct of a milk-producing cow is veal, its offspring.

Aaron Harmon is a Sol Pops Co-founder, LEED Accredited Professional, and Professor of Legal Writing at Lewis & Clark Law School.

SolPops.com | @solpops

Junk Mail Recycling Without the Bin

Cheryl Hilsenbeck

My mountain of junk mail has become a molehill!

About 5 years ago, a new thought wandered through my frazzled brain as I lugged another bin containing mostly junk mail to the curb for recycling. I was sick and tired of using time, space, and energy sifting through the steady, endless deluge of unsolicited information thrust upon me. I'd made routine requests to delete us from mailing lists, but had no measurable success.

"Why not mail it back to the people creating it?"

The next day I opened my new junk mail and found the predictable return envelope. You know the one I mean: the "No Postage Necessary" return envelope. I took the original envelope with my name and address, circled it with a bold marker, and wrote, "Please remove this name and address from your mailing list!"

Then I folded the outside envelope with my name and address circled, corralled the inserts, and stuffed everything compacted neatly into their provided return envelope. (Rumor has it, they pay by weight for return mail, but I don't know.)

Yes, it did take extra effort on my part for a short time, but here's the bottom line: My volume of junk mail has been reduced by about 90%! Evidently it is no longer cost effective to send junk to me.

I consider it a clear form of communication, and am happy they need not waste time, paper, or postage on an ungrateful recipient.

The time saved on junk mail has been invested in our business going paperless.

Consequently, The Bookkeeping Company is free to pursue our passionate commitment to help small business owners experience success. Our skills in financial detail are targeted to bring wisdom, clarity, security, and peace of mind to small business owners. We specialize in treating clients and employees like family, understanding no two are alike, and each one brings strengths and weaknesses to the table.

Cheryl Hilsenbeck is CFO at The Bookkeeping Company, LLC.
TBCinfo.com

The Problem with Paper

Layman L. Harang

It's easy, simple, cheap, and we all use it. In fact it is everywhere. So what is the big deal with paper?

The problem is the scale. Last year we—USA—used 100 million tons of the stuff and for all of the talk about recycling, paper currently constitutes the largest contribution to our landfills. Thirty-four percent of what we throw away is paper. The question is why. Is it the lack of alternate solutions? Hardly. Technical solutions are numerous and readily available. The entire Library of Congress is available online. Is it the cost? No again. Migrating to paperless formats has been proven time and time again to save money—a lot of money.

So what is the problem? Why is our consumption of paper going up, not down? In a world where we stay in touch via social media, texting and 24/7 global cell phones, we are addicted to the stuff.

The problem is us.

We get an important email and what do we do? We print the thing so that we can save it. An important document comes into the office and what is the first thing that happens? Someone ask for 10 copies. We show up at a staff meeting and everyone walks into the room with a copy of the agenda. We don't need the agenda, but we print it anyway. We do it because we can. We do it because it is cheap. We do it because we feel important carrying the stuff down the hallway. We utilize 21st century technology to communicate and then we rely on something that dates to 2nd century for safe-keeping. As ridiculous as it sounds, with all the gadgets and whiz bang methods of communicating, we are stuck on 1,800 year old technology for storage. We are stuck here at the detriment of the planet and our bottom lines.

What to do?

First, stop the madness. You don't really need 10 or 5 or even 2 copies of everything.

Second, get some help. There are technologies and processes that can be employed that can help virtually any business become paperless or at least less paper dependent. The challenge is in making the decision to begin.

The good news is that businesses all over town have begun and are succeeding. You can too.

Layman L. Harang leads The Karmann Group, a Portland consulting and software firm that assist in the transition from paper to more efficient and sustainable business methods.

KarmannGroup.com

2-8 Green Your Operations

For true sustainability to occur, business operations need to adapt, evolve and incorporate appropriate practices. The operation of your small business offers a multitude of opportunities for greening up. In fact, operations may be the best place to start the process.

What changes have you made in your business operations to include green practices? What were the biggest obstacles to incorporating sustainability into your operations and how did you overcome them? Who championed the shift in your business operations and how did they make it happen?

Minimize Meetings, Maximize Technology

Marlynn Schotland

Like many business owners, I am asked to participate in a large number of meetings. In my experience in corporate communications and as a serial entrepreneur, I've discovered that up to 90 percent of requested meetings are completely unnecessary. While the mid-century American institution known as the business lunch is still alive and well, and the 1990s surge of coffee meetings rages on, my experience is that cutting out a large percentage of in-person meetings greatly improves productivity, reduces cost, and minimizes a business's carbon footprint. All three benefits are critical in remaining a profitable, sustainable business in today's society, and all are easier to achieve thanks to technology.

When I have a 30-minute meeting, I know to schedule two hours to incorporate time for meeting prep, travel, parking, and time to settle back into the office and regain focus for what's next on the agenda. That's an hour and a half per meeting, wasted. With virtual meetings, I can schedule 2 to 4 per hour, often more than doubling my customer reach in the same amount of time. Less travel equals less environmental impact as well as cost reduction, which inevitably all leads to increased profits. What's good for the environment can, indeed, be good for business.

I won't argue that sometimes there is no replacement for the in-person meeting. However, ask yourself if the value of that meeting justifies the loss of productivity and the environmental impact of driving or flying. You'll find most issues can be handled via email, telephone, Skype, or even social media. If you've ever been to a conference having never met a soul in person prior to the conference, but having developed close relationships with attending colleagues via Twitter or Facebook, you understand the relationship power that is possible through technology.

As a native Portlander, I grew up practicing eco-friendly methods, so it was easy for me to transfer a lot of the day-to-day sustainable habits from home to work. However, I am also a very social person, and let's face it: I love the social and the food and drink benefits that come with many meetings. Although it took me a while to get used to this practice, the results speak for themselves: minimizing meetings and maximizing technology leads to a more sustainable, more productive, and more profitable business.

Marlynn Jayme Schotland is Owner of Urban Bliss, LLC, President of Mamapreneurs Inc. DBA The Power MOB, and Editor of Urban Bliss Life.

UrbanBlissDesign.com | @designmama

Sustainability as a Journey

Kevin Pile

I've spent 17 years questioning the state of the world, the disconnect between my personal ideals and my work, and corporate sustainability. My current project, Ecotrain Media Group, resulted from the trials and tribulations during these years' idealistic ecopreneurship: I've built a strong foundation in corporate sustainability through projects like eco-tourism resorts, renewable alternatives, portable power production, green cruise line certifications, environmental non-profit education, and permaculture garden design.

I look at sustainability from three different perspectives: societal, business, and personal. From a societal perspective, sustainable development entails improving quality of life and advancing appropriate technology and knowledge. From a business perspective, sustainable development encompasses increasing quality, lowering cost, and minimizing your future risk. From a personal perspective, sustainability is an entirely different subject.

Any ethical or social value you implement in your business will show financial returns over the long run. For instance, it's pretty straightforward to compare the up-front dollar cost of a renewable energy system and the number of years it would take to see a return compared to your current monthly power bill. However, it's often difficult to show a return on sustainable business practices. For example, as Hotel Director I would receive a case of Red Bull per week to reward crew members. I could not easily communicate a financial return on the switch from Red Bull to kombucha, a healthier alternative. In fact, I would be spending extra per drink. Not showing on the budget line were higher guest satisfaction scores, fewer job injuries, lower turnover rate, healthier crew, lower retraining costs, more productivity, etc.

I am enjoying my new social purpose. I founded Ecotrain Media Group to be an ongoing, sustainable business experiment. Upon founding and before sales or other traditional business start-up priorities, Ecotrain Media Group focused solely on sustainable practices. As an LLC with no outside investment, we could retain full control of decision-making. From there we continue to do as much as we can, including our Corporate Sustainability Bylaws and our Quarterly Sustainable Business Operations Report posted on our website. We break operations into 14 business departments, each of which we break down further into the most prominent sustainability perspectives: environmental values, social values, mind/body/soul values, financial values, localization values, political values, and natural values.

Kevin Pile is the founder of Ecotrain Media Group.
EcoTrainMediaGroup.com | @Ecotrain

Calibrate the Rainbow and See Green
Edward Flynn

Usually in business, the move to save resources and create environmentally conscientious processes is initiated by individuals whose smart thinking eventually percolates up to the rest of the organization.

Sometimes environmentalism is the unintended consequence of incompetent middle managers just trying to impress bosses.

I once worked in the digital retouching department of a large New York City-based ad agency. My department was managed by the epitome of do-nothing, unqualified dunderheads. Let's call him "Bob". How Bob ascended to manager, considering his sheer ineptitude and lack of skill, was always the big debate within our department. But what Bob lacked in ability he compensated with an overwhelming fascination for technology!

Helping his situation was his boss, "Ron", who was mostly too busy, either attending three-martini lunches or playing golf with the CFO, to be bothered with Bob. As long as Ron got a steady supply of baffling technological reports and purchase orders from Bob—with seemingly endless hours of research put into them—then Bob knew his phony baloney job was safe.

However, Ron, who also fell into his job without a clue as to what it entailed, relied on said technology reports to justify his own position to the agency's CFO.

One day, Bob submitted a report called "RGB Profiled Digital Workflows". In it, Bob boldly stated the agency needed to cast aside its old ways of CMYK proofing. Bob said the future was all about working in RGB! And that we should email files to clients who could then view the file on color-calibrated monitors. Upon approval, the file would then be printed using special printing profiles which converted the file to whatever end result color or format: magazine ads, newspaper ad, web banners, etc. Bob concluded his report with grand declarations on how much money and time it would save the agency and clients.

After reading this, Ron congratulated Bob on his genius and then ran to the CFO to reap the glory of the idea. Shortly after, the equipment needed was purchased and the process put in place.

Unfortunately, the clients were baffled by approving just pixels on a screen, so the whole idea momentarily collapsed. But once clients were trained by the agency, the plan flourished. Soon the amount of wasted paper, chemicals, and matchprints made was cut in half thanks to the use of Bob's RGB Digital Workflow.

Today, Bob is still a dufus, but he is a dufus who accidentally contributed to saving the environment.

Edward Flynn is a designer, web guy and videographer with far too much experience in the advertising and printing business.
UglyMugWorld.com | @uglymugagency

Growing and Staying Green

Alan Gunderson

Can you grow and stay green? At Package Containers, Inc. ("PCI"), we've spent five years expanding our internal recycling program while increasing sales, production, and profitability of our paper bag and wire tie lines used in the grocery, restaurant, bakery and wine industries. Additionally, we've maintained full employment and added a seasonal extra shift.

During this expansion, we've also decreased our waste and earned rebates for recycling production waste—a win-win for the environment and us! Here are a few tips based on what we've learned in "growing green":

- Encourage an employee who was passionate about sustainability to attend a Certified Master Recycler course so she could train other workers. (This program is sponsored by the City of Portland Bureau of Planning and Sustainability.)
- Join a business group dedicated to sustainable practices. If there isn't one in your area, start one! PCI belongs to the Sustainable Business Network of Portland.
- Assess your production and waste disposal practices and determine how close you can place scrap bins to your production machinery, thereby increasing efficiency and reducing transport time. As you grow, revamp floor layouts so the streamlined work flow continues to capture waste effectively.
- Design and designate a "Recycling Center" for information posting and collection, expanding the center as needed to recycle additional waste from increased production. Encourage employees to bring difficult-to-recycle items from home, offering to dispose of them. At PCI we dedicated a brightly painted, well-marked corner of our factory floor for this purpose.

- Sort production scrap into clearly marked bins that are emptied regularly, compacted, and taken to a predetermined storage area until ready for recycler pick-up. Specialized recyclable items should also have their own bins.

- When possible, reuse incoming packing materials for outgoing shipments. We decreased wood pallet purchases for shipping our finished products by recycling incoming pallets as they arrived with raw production materials. We now switch out incoming #1 or #2 wood pallets with lesser quality #3 pallets for materials storage. By using the better pallets for customer shipments, we have saved $4-$11 per pallet in overhead expense.

- Compost grass cuttings and landscape debris regularly and reuse the compost to keep outdoor plants and trees near your business green, fertilized and protected.

- Encourage employees to voice their own work-site sustainability ideas to get everyone involved. Start a green team and watch it grow!

Alan Gunderson is Art Director, Special Sales Manager, and Certified Master Recycler at Package Containers, Inc., in Canby, Oregon.

PackageContainers.com

Indulge Responsibly: Take Your Passion and Make It Green

Stacey Matney

I like shoes. Actually, I love shoes. So much so that when life afford me the opportunity to break out on my own, it was hard to think of anything better than owning my own shoe store. When I started getting serious about becoming an entrepreneur, beyond doing what I love, I also wanted to do what I loved responsibly. This left me with the question: Would I be able to apply the concepts of sustainability to a retail environment?

My husband, who has a background in organic produce, was the biggest champion of taking my idea for a sustainable shoe store to the next level. He helped me believe that you can take any idea and, through your operating practices, make it "green". At the time I created my business model, putting sustainability and shoes together was a new concept for the footwear industry as well as for the retail consumer. We called it "indulging responsibly".

We started making our concept sustainable through the planning of our business operations. We asked ourselves: How should we buy product and what should we buy? How should we build out our store to reduce our daily energy use and minimize our footprint? How should we run our daily operations to be sustainable?

Creativity was a key ingredient to taking our idea from everyday to green. Once we came up with a buying guide we called "Sustainable Ingredients Standards", which rates each product we sell on their environmental and social impact at the product and corporate levels, everything else came easily. We built out our storefront with all reclaimed materials, eliminated the need for trash service, reduced our energy usage through the use of LEDs, and started a shoe recycling program.

As a small, sustainable business, our biggest challenges are time and money. Making the sustainable choice is not always the cheapest or the easiest option. For us, the decision to be transparent about our operating practices has been the key to auditing ourselves and continuing to run our business as originally intended.

I am an entrepreneur. Instead of opening a shoe store, I opened an environmentally and socially responsibly shoe boutique.

Stacey Matney is a Portland native and the owner of Pie Footwear, an eco-conscious shoe boutique.

PieFootwear.net

Part 3: Prosperity

Wikipedia defines prosperity as the "state of flourishing, thriving, success or good fortune". Beyond economic factors, such as wealth, prosperity encompasses correlated elements, such as happiness and health. In business, prosperity goes beyond profit by taking a broader, systemic view of financial success.

How can sustainable practices reduce business expenses? What novel ways of sustainably generating revenue have proven to work? How has your company teamed up with others to take advantage of your respective special expertise, resources, experience, or scale? What does the transition from the profit motive to the prosperity mindset entail?

In Part 3, Portland's small-business leaders share stories about how they made sustainability work for them financially.

3-9 Reduce Cost

Sustainable practices tend to result in direct savings in many areas. Reducing your company's energy and material intensity can lower the cost of doing business—often dramatically—while leading to positive impacts in the People and Planet bottom lines. Sustainable practices can pay long-term dividends for everyone.

What have you done to reduce your expenditures by implementing environmentally or socially sustainable practices? How have you leveraged your cost savings to affect further change?

Sustainability as a Force for Success

Ken Hiatt

Sustainability is a thriving force. I learned early in my practice that I could leverage nearly any project for more value by applying sustainable principles. Such principles are defined by various existing frameworks such as The Natural Step, Triple Bottom Line, Industrial Ecology and Biomimicry. I like to educate with these frameworks to set a tone for an organic process that takes into consideration the entire business and integrates a sustainable mindset throughout the company.

My process is assessing where the company is today in relation to economy, product delivered and delivery systems. I examine the entire company, including executives, building/facilities, human resources, administration, marketing, information technology, and any current sustainability initiatives such as recycling or energy efficiency.

I engage with the company to look for "sustainability entry points", the traditional areas within the company that directly support business operations and have been identified for improvement. Then I match desired improvements against the sustainability assessment. I always find low hanging fruit in assessment areas that yield cost savings in energy efficiency, process efficiency, and transportation. When we align these initiatives to a project area there is an opportunity to introduce sustainable processes.

This process worked very well with a small technology company client. A sustainability vision was already established at the executive level. Their initiatives focused on purchasing electricity generated by wind power and an efficiency improvement process for their server farm. My assessment demonstrated a lack of metrics (data) to prove that these initiatives were adding value to the company and of periodic sustainability reporting.

I worked with them to design custom metrics that illustrated improvements against a baseline showing their efforts produced a reduction in energy use of 60% from their innovative server efficiency program over a 5-year period.

Besides identifying energy cost savings objectively, the real success story came when the client reported the story to stakeholders. Traditional stakeholders are generally internal constituents, stockholders, and boards of directors. Stakeholders for a sustainable company include the "traditionals" plus customers, vendors, and community. Transparency is foundational to sustainability. Communicating in this way resulted in a dramatic increase in customer acquisitions.

As we continue to work together, we are building deeper sustainability reporting that will be used to further drive business decisions, cost savings, and, ideally, more customers.

Ken Hiatt is a sustainability thought leader and Founder of Peraska, which helps companies implement sustainability for compliance, competitive advantage, cost reduction, and better performance.
Peraska.com | @kenhiatt

Time-Tested Measures for Reducing Costs

Kate McNulty

Part of the art of management is being able to identify the most efficient strategies for reducing expenses without compromising the future of the business. Business owners often delay applying cost controls until their company is under stress. However, it is critically important that decision-makers in this situation avoid emotional reactivity.

Businesses that succeed despite the challenges of lean times and scarcity typically do so because their owners are making decisions based on data. When the business owner routinely collects and monitors data about expenses, income, and cash flow, either on their own or with a bookkeeper's help, they are equipped to respond to fluctuations and drops in revenue. These events are routine and unavoidable, and are not a cause for panic.

The business owner who is inexperienced or unprepared may be tempted to cut marketing expenses and staffing, or to skimp on costs of service or production. However, the risk of sacrificing volume of business, quality, or customer experience does not justify reducing costs in these areas. It's always better to maintain a consistent level of services and reduce costs than it is to cut back on service or quality. Although employees are the largest fixed costs for almost every business, staffing cutbacks can result in poor morale for employees, causing a spillover of negativity in the day-to-day operations of the business.

Referring to a business plan, income goals and marketing targets allows the business owner to keep focused during difficult times and figure out how to cut waste or control expenses.

Rather than cutting back on marketing or reducing employee hours, business owners may find surprising savings through employing a combination of these tactics:

- Negotiate with your bank to reduce overdraft fees and penalties and get better credit card processing fees.
- Avoid tax penalties by making quarterly payments on time.
- Request monthly invoices from suppliers or contractors to minimize processing costs.
- Review IT costs and seek opportunities to save by using online services with free upgrades; involve an IT consultant or staff in budget discussions so they partner with you in efforts to minimize costs.
- Increase customer satisfaction by seeking feedback; build in reward programs for loyalty and repeat business as appropriate to setting.

These measures are unobtrusive and lasting in their benefits, averting a crisis atmosphere, and steadily building a healthy cash flow. Keep calm and rely on data for success.

Kate McNulty is the owner of Small Business Money Tree, helping entrepreneurs grow and prosper. She is the author of Easy Business Cash Flow.

SmallBusinessMoneyTree.com | @biz_money_tree

Think Small

Kat Schon

My partner and I started our business selling used store fixtures in a much smaller space with a much smaller budget and we were the staff. In the beginning, every decision, no matter how small, was important and we were green because it made the best budgetary sense. We reused packing materials, bags, boxes, hardware, and whatever else we could because it meant not having to buy those things new. What we didn't reuse, we recycled, even if that meant breaking a giant showcase down into its smallest parts. It was simple math: The less we put into our dumpster, the less it cost to have it emptied.

We also saved money by using recycled letterhead and envelopes (printing invoices and correspondence on the blank side), refilling our ink cartridges rather than buying new, and turning the heat off a half an hour before leaving. We grouped deliveries to the same general area to reduce mileage and didn't deliver on Fridays when trucks were more likely to get stuck in traffic. We learned that small economies add up: The trick is to remember those lessons as your budget increases.

Now, we support 12 employees, own two of the three buildings we occupy, and have become a place for small business owners to get advice and support, as well as buy, sell, and rent new, used, and custom store fixtures. Our original business practices are still in place: We use old letterhead, reuse everything we possibly can, and recycle the rest.

What has changed? As our budget increased, we found that not only could we do more to help the environment but that we wanted to do more. We had solar panels installed on the roof, motion detector lights installed in the back warehouse, and we're branching out to help larger stores introduce store fixture recycling programs.

My partner and I and all of our staff are dedicated to reducing the impact our business has on the environment. The green economies we used in the beginning out of necessity, are also part of what helped us to thrive. Being green has become an integral part of our business. Our mantra is, "Reduce, Reuse, Recycle, Repeat". We take pride in how little our stores send to the landfill because at the end of the day, it's all about the little things—in business, as well as life.

Kat Schon thinks playtime is key and co-owns, with her partner Penney Stephenson, a giant dog, a pair of kayaks, a casita, and Portland Store Fixtures.

PortlandStoreFixtures.com

Technology Makes Sustainability Profitable!

Janeese Jackson

Sustainability is a loaded term. I'm confused, bemused and amused by vernacular at times. I hope you'll allow me to discover what I mean by sustainability as I write this article. Webster defines "sustain" as to "maintain, prolong, endure, withstand, or suffer". Suffering aside, I'm all for prolonging anything I perceive as positive and ending anything I perceive as negative.

You can argue the economics of sustainability all day but none of it matters if it doesn't further your business objective. I'm a seasoned—that's the way people of a certain age like to refer to themselves—business person, who has run an independent real estate business since 1985. There was no internet (gasp!), no cell phones (double gasp!), and I remember the day I won a multiple offer situation for my buyer client because I faxed my offer instead of Fed-Ex over-nighting it to an out-of-state seller. I am now and have always been a fan of new technology. Love it, love it, love it!

But, I digress. Sustainability is now a multi-tasking term. I've watched as the world matured and the expectations increased. I've watched the integration of "use and re-use" become commonplace. I've seen the world change from having to drive across town to recycle to urban garbage companies offering recycling. You're now politically incorrect if you don't recycle.

What does sustainability mean to my business? It means print is dead. Yes, dead! I'm not saying people don't and shouldn't read. I have a Kindle and am a voracious online reader. All the statisticians agree that over 90% of buyers start their search on the internet. Why waste time on print venues that don't connect able buyers with willing sellers? You are still spending money on marketing your brand. Your blog and your online presence cost money.

But, this type of marketing allows for less of an ecological footprint. I've watched over the years as our realtor information-sharing went from large phone-book sized publications to Multiple Listing websites, as cell phone voicemails replaced office receptionists and paper messages, as multiple web presences replaced newspaper ads, as company publications are being replaced by individual agent blog sites, as fax (and often phone) are being replaced by email, and as paper flyers are being replaced by perma-flyers. None of this disturbs me. It's use without having to think about re-use.

Janeese Jackson is Principal Broker at Real Estate Resource. Her job is expert service to you, using 25 years of experience to help you achieve your real estate goals.

FabulousPortland.com | @janeesejackson

3-10 Shift Your Business Model

Generating revenue through sustainable, future-oriented innovation must also meet social and environmental goals. Today, many companies—start-ups and established firms alike—include social profit in their pursuit of financial profitability.

How have you developed or changed your business model to incorporate sustainability? What novel business models have you applied in your business? How has your business focused around a social or environmental mission?

Keeping It Real: Tips for Green Business People
David Vanadia

Make Sure You Can Sustain Being Sustainable

Don't build your business around being green unless you love it, live it, and can keep it up for the long haul.

Does Being Green Make You Money?

You're in business to generate capital. Even non-profits need income. Being staunch in your green ways can sometimes hinder your ability to make a buck. Try to set it up so that when the time to choose comes, the green option earns you more money.

How Does Your Sustainability Benefit Your Customers?

Whatever the reason, knowing the value of your sustainability will make it easier for you to communicate it to your customers and thus generate more sales.

Brag, Don't Promise

Someone will always point out how you are using excessive resources. If you've advertised yourself as a green business but end up doing something that's not sustainable, people can question your integrity. That said, when your company does something right, tell the world! What's the difference between bragging and advertising? Bragging happens after you've done something, while advertising makes promises before you do anything.

Reward Sustainability

People need incentive, so decorate the sustainable route with rewards that people value. If sustainability earns money, it becomes its own reward.

Word-of-Merch?

Your key chain has a company logo on it and you got it at a trade show, right? Please! Concentrate your investments on making a positive impact on your customer's life and they will sing your praises. Word-of-mouth marketing is still the most sustainable and believable way to generate business. If you have to give something away, gift useful samples of your product or service.

"Green Product" Is an Oxymoron

Designing a new widget made out of sustainable materials is—wait, we don't need more widgets! Green stuff is not the answer to the problem of too much stuff.

Experience Trumps All

The "been there, done that, got the T-shirt" paradigm is so 1980s. Make people feel special, amazing, renewed, smart, or happy and they will come back again and again. People always return to the places where they have found value. Today's motto should be, "Been there, done that, let's go back and do it again!"

Integrate

For most businesses, being green is an added value. It won't happen overnight, but the more you seamlessly integrate being green into your work, the easier it is to sustain. You can't always be green but you can always try.

David Vanadia works with stories.
Vanadia.com | @vanadia

Lean Times Bear Fruit

Jane Pellicciotto

A bad economy begs rethinking and repurposing. I once viewed my lack of employees or sexy office space as a liability. But with a lean lifestyle and business, I could clarify purpose, feed passions, sharpen skills and cultivate connections—ingredients for an enriching business down the road.

Clarify Purpose

My work has always reflected a commitment to brand and market organizations and businesses that provide services or products for the common good. The bad economy and a desire for change and improvement forced me to assess what I wanted to do most and with whom, which meant shutting some doors, deepening involvement in key areas, and having more respect for my talents and skills.

Feed Passions

The kindred aspects of food—fairness, health, local economies, cooking, culture, land use, and policy—hold great interest for me. This passion developed like a slow-growing seed, extending to collaborations with chefs, writing opportunities, and a personal project—a year-long visual log of fresh produce that tracks my expenses on local versus non-local food. This project feeds the twin desires of structure and creative expression, while literally putting my money where my mouth is. A second passion—writing—saw the light in the last few years, and flourished.

Sharpen Skills

My writing efforts had been limited to the eyes of few. I wanted to enrich my business, and that of clients, through more than images— meaningful, strategic content. This meant writing often to develop a cache of published work. I started a blog, wrote for the farmer's market, took a powerful writing workshop, and developed communications for sustainable design events—all of which require research, tight editing, persuasive language and interviewing subjects. But the path was not always clear or linear!

Cultivate Meaningful Connections

If you work alone, you have to connect with others. But to conserve your energy and time for the right impact, these connections should feed your soul and business and reflect your values. The more clarity you have, the easier it is to know which connections will benefit you most. For me, it has come down to a business networking group, a writing group, a sustainable design team, the farmer's market and other food connections, and related social media outlets. This is quite enough. But they all feed off each other, making the transitions from work to life more seamless.

Jane Pellicciotto is sole proprietor of Allegro Design. She uses wise strategies with enriching results for good businesses.
Allegro-Design.com | @allegrojane

Sustainability Seminar

Tony Koach

I would love to teach the seminar called "How to Build a Sustainable House in an Unsustainable Market"—the seminar I wish I had taken prior to starting construction on two Gold LEED Certified houses in March 2008.

I had secured financing for the project through a lender in Seattle. I was confident that the loan documents were on their way to closing, so I got the excavator and the foundation contractors going. Ten days after we started construction I got a letter from my lender saying they had closed their doors. No money. No explanation. Current rumors about the pending collapse of Bear Stearns may have been the reason my Seattle lender pulled the plug.

At this point in the seminar, we would have a break out section titled, "What would you do now?" You have two lots with big holes in them, sewer and water lines installed, and foundations about to be poured. In 45 days you will owe the sub contractors $35,000 that you don't have.

My concept was to build a simple contemporary house with a flex space that could be used as an office, shop, family room, a 3rd bedroom, or a legal studio apartment. The house was designed to meet LEED criteria established by the United States Green Building Council. LEED guidelines go beyond energy efficiencies and the use of recycled products. They include criteria such as: Who is on the design team? Are you digging up farmland to build on? Are you near a park and public transit? Can you walk to the store?

I was confident we had the right product for the right price. So I found a new local lender and kept building. My lender agreed, "How bad can the economy get?" (title of next breakout session.)

Bad.

The houses took a year to sell. They lost 35% of the pre-Bear Stearns appraisal. Ouch! But the point of the story is that even when trying and believing earnestly in doing the right thing, you never know how it is going to turn out. But you have to keep trying. Analyze, decide, adjust, invent. Sustainability isn't a quantity or a calculation. It's understanding the biology and physics of our endeavors.

We did the right thing. A win for the environment. A win for the buyers of the homes. And a very expensive learning experience.

Tony Koach of Koach Development is a developer, architect, and contractor specializing in facilities for healthcare and science (and housing when the market recovers).

KoachDevelopment.com

Sustainable Branding: It May Not Be What You Think

Rich Bruer

You're a small business and can't afford branding because, well, you're small. Branding is for big companies with giant advertising budgets. Besides, you're about sustainability. Branding is crass commercialism.

Fair enough. But being small and sustainable doesn't exempt you from possessing a brand in need of attention. You have customers, prospects, employees, suppliers, and other stakeholders. That means you have an image. It may be based on people's direct interaction with your company, what they heard from others (including your competitors) or what they saw in the media. And that image—favorable or not—is your brand.

The question isn't whether you can afford branding. It's whether you can afford to ignore your brand.

If you see your business through the lens of sustainability, you know business as usual no longer cuts it. Sustainability asks you to look anew at all your practices and operations. What often gets overlooked is your brand and its effect on your business.

My work is helping businesses rethink branding. From the outside, your brand is the image others have of your business. From the inside, it's your promise to stakeholders—what you stand for that creates business distinction and relevance.

Conventional branding hinges on image creation, through clever design, marketing and communications. Sustainable branding stresses the promise fulfilled, through all your actions and practices as a business. You might call it living your brand. Seen this way, branding isn't simply what you're communicating. It's who you're being.

Sustainable businesses care deeply about who they're being. They want to be—and be experienced as—innovators, good citizens, responsible employers, ethical competitors, and environmental stewards.

Conventional branding seeks to build an image or manufacture an experience that sells. It's often expensive, superficial and manipulative.

Sustainable branding is about letting your actions lead your words. It's about knowing your reason for being as a business. What sets you apart. Why you matter. It's about engaging your employees in your brand's creation and meaning. It's not about the size of your business or your advertising budget. It's about making a promise—and keeping it.

Rich Bruer is Principal of R.Bruer Company, a sustainable branding firm, and co-founder and former principal of McClenahan Bruer Communications, a tech PR and ad agency.

RBruer.com | @rbruer

Environmental Adaptation: Lessons from Nature for Better Business

Mike Johnson

Necessity is the mother of invention.

When I started the ReDirect Guide ten years ago, it was out of an urgent need to change people's behaviors and redirect them to more responsible options. In the Portland of 2000, that meant knocking on doors to find my allies in sustainability and then releasing the area's first comprehensive, independently certified guide to green companies. The guide was, and still is, free and accessible to anyone looking to make a change. From the beginning, it was clear to me that my company existed because of an ecosystem of inter-dependent and ever-changing community members and businesses. I've learned a lot of other lessons from nature's systems since that first year, and because of it, my business has changed dramatically.

Here are a few things I make sure to keep in mind:

Cultivation

Don't get ahead of yourself. Keep your mission in mind, be patient, and remember that where you're starting from is not where you're going to go. Working from a realistic and approachable starting point makes my work accessible to newcomers and green experts alike, in the hopes that we can all move forward toward better innovation.

Adaptation

ReDirect responds to changes in our environment in order to survive. In the last few years, we've gone from being a print-only resource to being a true multimedia network. We are available through many entry points, and this ensures we stay relevant and accessible.

Interdependence

You can't do it alone. Change toward environmental stewardship and collective consciousness requires working together. Because of this, we've begun to leverage our relationships with companies and organizations to connect them directly with one another to solve problems together. With our collective strengths, we begin to eliminate our weaknesses.

Restoration

Heal the damage. In order to grow, businesses must not only create less damage to the environment, but must take restorative measures to sustain our place in the ecosystem. Two years ago, I brought to life a restorative program for ReDirect: a carbon offsetting credit card that encourages responsible purchasing from green companies, and offsets the impact of any purchase, regardless of the product or service. It is my sincere hope that I can continue to implement strategies focused on restoration, not just lessening our collective impact.

Mike Johnson is the founder of ReDirect Guide, a business network that independently certifies, promotes, and connects local green companies in Oregon, Washington, Utah, and Colorado.
ReDirectGuide.com | @redirectguide

3-11 Collaborate

Companies don't exist in a vacuum. They're embedded in larger economic and social systems. Long-term success has come to mean collaboration with suppliers, service providers, and even competitors to achieve common goals. Working together can bring tremendous benefits to all parties as well as the world at large.

How have you put collaboration to work in your business? What have you achieved through collaboration that you couldn't have accomplished alone? What methods, processes, or tools have you used to join forces with fellow business leaders?

Collaboration, Transparency, and Metrics Foster Sustainable Change

Dave R. Meyer

A few years ago, I assisted a water utility in implementing a sustainability focused initiative based on the International Organization for Standardization ("ISO") 14001-2004 Environmental Management System standard. Many public and private organizations operate in functional silos, often don't coordinate well, communicate effectively or run efficiently. Creating a triple bottom line-focused organization requires that all parts work together—like organs of a living being. This utility was inefficient with taxpayer dollars and under intense public scrutiny to improve its operations. It was not healthy.

Through the two-year journey with the company, I worked hard to know each of its parts, how they interacted, where the trouble spots were, and where good health was. The goal was to build a holistic, sustainable organization that capitalized on its best assets: the staff. To be truly optimized and efficient, it was vital to shore up operational weaknesses. The program focused on new communication techniques, champion-building, public environmental awareness, and creating a culture of continuous change management. Public agencies are often stuck in a business-as-usual ("BAU") mindset. The ISO 14001-2004 program and other internal performance turn-around initiatives required moving beyond the BAU mindset. Key steps and measures that contributed to the turnaround included the following spheres:

1. *Environmental*: Early establishment of cross-functional performance improvement teams that focused on key measurable indicators, e.g. energy efficiency, resource management, and waste reduction.

2. *Operational*: Collaborative fact-finding, problem resolution and decision-making around staff utilization and scheduling, resource optimization, asset management, emergency response, and predictive maintenance.

3. *Social*: Proactive external public education and awareness campaigns at city-run facilities to engage community support related to natural resource management and watershed conservation efforts; employee initiatives that encouraged buy-in and financial rewards for cost saving measures and led to a reduced environmental footprint.

The organization achieved its ISO 14001-2004 certification, garnered prestigious national awards, and saved the City over $100 million in 5 years.

After the certification award, a 30-year veteran of the department approached me. He hadn't believed in the programs value at the start—maybe because of his BAU approach, or maybe he didn't like change. He said, "Dave, I want to thank you. You made us do something that we would not have done ourselves". That is what cultural change is all about. For once, I was speechless.

The keys to the success of this sustainability program and others like it are: cross-functional collaboration and employee input (early and often), early stakeholder collaboration, and metrics. These ingredients alone will go a long way toward laying the foundation for long term success of your organization's sustainability initiatives and going beyond business-as-usual.

Dave R. Meyer is VP of Sustainable Economic and Environmental Development Solutions (SEEDS) Global Alliance, assisting organizations on business process improvement, environmental sustainability, green supply chain, and regulatory compliance management.

ValueStream2009.WordPress.com | @DRMeyer1

3-12 Manage Change

Change is hard, even when you embrace it. Changing a business can be even more challenging because you must motivate a multitude of stakeholders and alter many processes and habits. Aiming to change your business toward sustainability is a long-term commitment.

How have you made the case for sustainability to your business partners, employees, or customers? What has worked in expanding mindsets from narrow profit to broader prosperity? What methods or tools have you used to manage change in your small business?

Change Happens

William Metzker

My interest in the world's environment began years ago, with the book "Silent Spring", in which Rachel Carson detailed the horrific effects of DDT on the ecosystem. It took 10 more years for the United States to ban DDT.

In 1970, I was an early organizer of Earth Day events. But the rainforests still burned, geysers of oil pumped, coal burned, the air fouled, and so on. Nothing changed. The fight against apathetic inertia became more draining than advocating the cause.

Chaos Theory suggests that a shift in the wind from a butterfly's wings has profound effects that are not immediately obvious. At the Earth Advantage Institute's Sustainability Training for Real Estate Professionals continuing education class, a revelation came to me that small changes each of us made could have an enormous effect. While I couldn't do much about atmospheric carbon hovering at 390 parts per million, I could change the microsystem I lived in.

I founded Terradigm Real Estate in 2010 with the intent of offering an option of fee-based consultancy in addition to the usual commission-based model—a big change for real estate sales. Because we were already trying to be different, adding sustainability services was a natural. But what became suddenly clear, to paraphrase Chekhov, was the imperative of incorporating environmentally responsible practices, not just during work hours, but always.

Certification as an Earth Advantage broker and membership in the Energy Trust of Oregon's trade ally network stitches Terradigm into the sustainability fabric that builders, architects, lenders, and others are weaving for Portland.

Our best practices include using Docusign, where most real estate contracts can be written, signed, and stored online. We can be almost paperless. "Almost" because of some lender and state requirements.

A minimum of $150 from every transaction is donated to not-for-profit groups with environmental associations.

Because of the "Beyond 2020 Unconference", Terradigm can network with like-minded business professionals, from accountants to communications people, to mortgage lenders and title companies, and have professionals to refer our clients to.

In my Orenco Station neighborhood, our team of Home Owners Association board members, owners, and our community manager charted 377 owners on a path to sustainability. Community practices now incorporate solar, landscape, and water-use guidelines. A library of sustainable building products and practices is under development.

A future challenge: How can the initial cost of sustainability be breeched so that the "green" life cycle benefits can accrue to low- and middle-income people? A solution may lie in creating a not-for-profit group to rehabilitate foreclosed homes sustainably and make them available to moderate income people.

William Metzker is the principal broker, owner and night custodian of Terradigm Real Estate Consultancy.
TerradigmRealEstate.com | @mrliam

Individual Progress in Waste Paper Recovery

Benjamin Brink

Do you find yourself getting into arguments or being discontent when promoting green processes? I have. The eighth dwarf, "Cranky", following Snow White's seven dwarves, was becoming my more popular nickname. The mark was true enough. I found myself cranky, especially after trying to green in new areas based on negative feedback and unresponsiveness to the effort. My personal mantra became, "Why am I meeting such resistance to this obviously green action?"

A green habit out of sorting the trash can have fringe benefits. Whether sheltered by other scraps of life from being drenched with mixed foodstuffs and coffee grounds dumped from the bottom of mugs at the end of a day's work, or contrasted with the handwritten sentence in red ink and wrapped by uncharacteristically doodled quotation marks, a torn and crinkled strip of paper caught my attention. It read:

"The mind has a place in practical life, but its role begins after the heart has had its say."—Meher Baba

The answer to my question was staring back at me as if the universe had just handed me a fortune without the cookie!

Had I listened more to others, I would have realized what was meant when I was described as "obstinate" (before being named Cranky). I was not considering the dispositions of others and listening to them and their values and motivations. Essentially, I was imposing my will on others instead of discussing my perception of a legitimate green issue. No wonder my colleagues and friends disparaged green initiatives in my presence. I had become a beacon of intolerance regardless of the motive. Thankfully, I listened to the scrap paper!

The role of the mind begins after the heart has had its say. The heart represents compassion, thoughtfulness and patience—kindness. The heart should not be confused with emotionality, oversensitivity, and zeal to the point of fanaticism. Now I know this.

Ironically, since Cranky is gone, there's more greening going on than I could have imagined. Locally, the best of the green ways are growing cooperatively and spreading by example—without my effort. How sustainable is that!

Benjamin Brink is a twenty-first century diagnostic archeo-anthropologist, survivor, visiting.
dekkaSupply.com

Conclusion: Toward the Social Book

Peter Korchnak and Megan Strand

Thank you for reading "The Portland Bottom Line". We enjoyed putting the book together and sharing this unique collection of Portland's sustainable business practices. Never again will this group of contributors come together in a single book (though we do hope that many will return for volume two).

While your head may now be swimming with ideas to implement in your own small business, we'd like to share what we've learned about crowdsourced book creation.

- A collaborative book takes more—effort, time, passion—than you might think. It's a beast, but it's the most exciting of beasts to have around.
- The awareness—interest—desire—action sequence of engagement applies just like for any other product. The main hump is in the middle, between interest and desire. In particular, word of mouth by contributors helps. Once the momentum gathers and the project tips, which can take a while, you're rolling.
- A crowd requires coordination. A successful collaborative project needs a dedicated manager to make sure all contributors fulfill their agreements. The closer the deadline, the better the compliance.
- Writing is intimidating to many. Doubly so when you include the word "publish". The permanence of a book is intriguing, scary, and exciting.

The definition and the medium of the book are undergoing a radical transformation. The social book—a collaborative, crowdcreated volume that benefits a cause, like "The Portland Bottom Line"—has sparked our passion for playing a role in the process. What's better than sharing your story with others in a book that makes a difference in your community?

Join us in making your story matter, as we breathe life into the social book at GoodBookery, a venture that has grown out of "The Portland Bottom Line".

Thank you.

Peter Korchnak explores the intersection of marketing and sustainability at Semiosis Communications, and collaborative book creation at GoodBookery.
SemiosisCommunications.com and GoodBookery

Megan Strand is a project manager and creative communicator. At InCouraged Communications, she spotlights, connects, and supports businesses that are doing well by doing good.
InCouraged.com | @meganstrand

Contributors

Meet the contributors of "The Portland Bottom Line":

David Anderson (p. 37) is Principal of Canvas Dreams, a sustainable Web hosting provider, which uses renewable energy and a certified B Corporation Web host.
CanvasDreams.com | @canvasdreams

Susan Bender Phelps (p. 29) is a professional mentoring and leadership development expert. She speaks about and teaches skills that lead to breakthrough performance and dynamic career growth.
OdysseyMentoring.com | @OdysseyMentor

Beatrice Benne (p. 13) is the owner of Soma Integral Consulting, a consulting firm that helps resolve adaptive challenges by transforming and designing purposeful, conscious organizations, while focusing on the well-being of ecosystems.
BeatriceBenne.com | @bcbenne

Benjamin Brink (p. 133) is a twenty-first century diagnostic archeo-anthropologist, survivor, visiting.
DekkaSupply.com

Rich Bruer (p. 121) is Principal of R.Bruer Company, a sustainable branding firm, and co-founder and former principal of McClenahan Bruer Communications, a tech PR and ad agency.
Rbruer.com | @rbruer

Caleb Bushner (p. 73) is a strategy and marketing change agent at From The Rooftops, a Portland-based brand strategy firm. He is also an unrepentant athlete and nerd.
FromTheRooftops.us | @calebbushner

Jonathan Davis (p. 23) is the Founder of GreenPosting.org.
GreenPosting.org | @GreenPosting

Tom Dwyer (p. 41) is the owner of Tom Dwyer Automotive Services.
TomDwyer.com

Janelle Fendall Baglien (p. 17) is president of Studio Art Direct, which provides turnkey corporate art programs created by regional artists and which is considered to be the nation's largest source for art by Portland-area artists.
StudioArtDirect.com

Edward Flynn (p. 95) is a designer, artist, web guy, and videographer with far too much experience in the advertising and printing business.
UglyMugWorld.com | @uglymugagency

Jennifer Forti (p. 45) is the founder of *the people's republic of portland.*
thepeoplesrepublicofportland.com | @theprop

Doug and MacKenzie Freeman (p. 57) are co-owners of Ideascape and Arnold Creek Productions, a sustainability media production company whose educational videos have won awards, including a Portland BEST, and been shown at film festivals around the world.
IdeascapeInc.com and ArnoldCreekProductions.com

Perry Gruber (p. 51) is Co-founder / CEO of NedWater, the world's first cause-driven drinking water company.
NedWater.net | @ned_perry

Alan Gunderson (p. 97) is Art Director, Special Sales Manager and Certified Master Recycler at Package Containers, Inc., in Canby, Oregon.
PackageContainers.com

Layman L. Harang (p. 87) leads The Karmann Group, a Portland consulting and software firm that assist in the transition from paper to more efficient and sustainable business methods.
KarmannGroup.com

Aaron Harmon (p. 83) is a Sol Pops co-founder, LEED Accredited Professional, and Professor of Legal Writing at Lewis & Clark Law School.
SolPops.com | @solpops

Betsy Henning (p. 67) is Principal of AHA!, a strategic communications firm with expertise in writing.
AHA-writers.com | @AHAwriters

Ken Hiatt (p. 105) is the founder of Peraska, where he helps companies implement sustainability for compliance, competitive advantage, cost reduction, and better performance.
Peraska.com | @kenhiatt

Cheryl Hilsenbeck (p. 85) is CFO at The Bookkeeping Company.
TBCinfo.com

Lisa Holmes (p. 81) is a principal at Yulan Studio, a design firm specializing in web, interactive, and print.
YulanStudio.com | @LisaDHolmes

Noland Hoshino (p. 59) is Givologist, Cause Enthusiast, and Chief Social Media Strategist at [B]cause Media Social Media Communciations.
BCauseMedia.com | @NolandHoshino

Janeese Jackson (p. 111) is Principal Broker at Real Estate Resource.   Her job is expert service to you, using 25 years of experience to help you achieve your real estate goals.
FabulousPortland.com | @janeesejackson

Mike Johnson (p. 123) is the founder of ReDirect Guide, a comprehensive sustainable business network that independently certifies, promotes, and connects local green companies in Oregon, Washington, Utah, and Colorado.

ReDirectGuide.com | @redirectguide

Tony Koach (p. 119) of Koach Development is a developer, architect, and contractor specializing in facilities for healthcare and science (and housing when the market recovers).

KoachDevelopment.com

Peter Korchnak (pp. 7 and 135) explores the intersection of marketing and sustainability at Semiosis Communications, and collaborative book creation at GoodBookery.

SemiosisCommunications.com and GoodBookery.com

Stacey Matney (p. 99) is a Portland native and the owner of Pie Footwear, an eco-conscious shoe boutique.

PieFootwear.net

Glenn Maynard, LPC, (p. 43) has extensive experience in administrative finance. He owns Portland Coaching and Counseling Center and specializes in addiction recovery.

PortlandCoachingandCounseling.com | @PDX_Counseling

Tess McBride (p. 77) is the communication and media outreach coordinator for Visual F/X Salon, a graduate student at PSU, a recycle nut, and a nature lover.

VisualFXSalon.com | @visualfxsalon

Kate McNulty (p. 107) is the owner of Small Business Money Tree, helping entrepreneurs grow and prosper. She is the author of "Easy Business Cash Flow".

SmallBusinessMoneyTree.com | @biz_money_tree

William Metzker (p. 131) is the principal broker, owner and night custodian of Terradigm Real Estate Consultancy.

TerradigmRealEstate.com | @mrliam

Dave R. Meyer (p. 127) is VP of Sustainable Economic and Environmental Development Solutions (SEEDS) Global Alliance, assisting organizations on business process improvement, environmental sustainability, green supply chain, and regulatory compliance management.

ValueStream2009.wordpress.com | @DRMeyer1

Lindsey Newkirk (p. 69) is the owner of Elysium Events, an event greening company that focuses on zero waste. She has helped her clients reach recovery rates of 66-98%.

ElysiumEventsLLC.com

Jane Pellicciotto (p. 117) is sole proprietor of Allegro Design. She uses wise strategies with enriching results for good businesses.

Allegro-Design.com | @allegrojane

Kevin Pile (p. 93) is the founder of Ecotrain Media Group.

EcoTrainMediaGroup.com | @Ecotrain

Mitch Rofsky (p. 75) is President of Better World Club.

BetterWorldClub.com

Mike Russell (p. 39) defends the reader's intelligence, champions his client's message, and conspires to promote the sustainability conversation.

PivotalWriting.com

Thaddeus Ruyer (p. 19) is architect, real estate broker, developer, human spirituality-consciousness apprentice, artist, sculptor, and musician.

Kat Schon (p. 109) thinks playtime is key and co-owns, with her partner Penney Stephenson, a giant dog, a pair of kayaks, a Casita, and Portland Store Fixtures.
PortlandStoreFixtures.com

Marlynn Jayme Schotland (p. 91) is Owner of Urban Bliss, LLC, President of Mamapreneurs Inc. DBA The Power MOB, and Editor of Urban Bliss Life.
UrbanBlissDesign.com | @designmama

Brian C. Setzler, MBA, CPA, (p. 65) is Founder and CEO at TriLibrium, a certified B-Corp public accounting firm, and a lecturer at the Bainbridge Graduate Institute.
TriLibrium.com | @GreenCPA

Kaya Singer (p. 53) is the owner of Awakening Business Solutions and the author of "Clear Your Focus Grow Your Business."
AwakeningBusiness.com

Sharon Soliday (p. 27) is a happy, powerless visionary.
TheHelloFoundation.com

Renee Spears (p. 49) is President of Rose City Mortgage, the nation's 1st socially responsible mortgage company, named by Oregon Business Magazine the state's #1 Small and #4 Green Company.
RoseCityMtg.com | @RoseCityMrtg

Megan Strand (p. 135) is a project manager and creative marketer. At InCouraged Communications she spotlights, connects, and supports businesses that are doing well by doing good.
InCouraged.com | @meganstrand

Amber Turner (p. 15) is a natural match-maker at Living Room Realtors, bringing homes and people together for lasting memories. She is also the founder of GreenPDX, which meets monthly for home tours or guest speaking events.
GreenPDX.com

David Vanadia (p. 115) works with stories.
Vanadia.com | @vanadia

Jennie Vinson (p. 55) is the owner of Mission First Marketing, a native Oregonian, and a creative marketing strategist working with mission-driven businesses in Portland and beyond.
MissionFirstMarketing.com | @missionfirst

Darcy Winslow (p. 5) is the founder and CEO of DSW Collective.
DSWCollective.com | @DSWCollective

Judith Yamada (p. 21) is an advocate for family farms, using her culinary training and experience to teach seasonal, sustainable food purchasing and preparation.
PortlandHomeCooking.com

Justin Yuen (p. 33) is President of FMYI, a collaboration software company, and a change agent.
FMYI.com | @FMYI

Robert Zahrowski (p. 31) provides advice on strategic planning, organizational development, process redesign, and productivity improvements to a wide variety of businesses.
RMZahrowski.com

Take Action!

This volume is just the beginning for "The Portland Bottom Line". Based on feedback, we're already planning the second volume, to be published in November 2011!

In the meantime:

- **Visit PortlandBottomLine.com**, where everything related to "The Portland Bottom Line" lives its digital existence.
- **Subscribe to the site via RSS or email** to get book updates, testimonials, contributor and sale information, and other good stuff.
- **Comment** on posts on the site.
- **Share your story** of implementing sustainable business practices you learned from the book, on the Your Story page.
- **Buy another copy** of the book to share with a friend on colleague. Better yet, buy five—it's for a good cause.
- **Learn more about Mercy Corps Northwest**, the book's beneficiary at MercyCorpsNW.org. Theycre good people helping other good people start and grow their own businesses.
- **Browse each contributor's website**, listed under each chapter and in the Contributors section. Learn more about their companies and practices, reach out to them for more information, or visit them in person.
- **Email us** at editors@portlandbottomline.com with any questions or suggestions.

Actions speak louder than (written) words!

Acknowledgments

Peter Korchnak would like to thank, for inspiration, support, encouragement, and hard work:

- Lindsay Sauvé
- Megan Strand
- Kelly Quashnie
- Mike Russell
- Heather Schiffke
- Each and every contributor of "The Portland Bottom Line" as well as everyone who didn't make it to this volume (see you in the next one!)
- Drew McLellan and Gavin Heaton at "Age of Conversation"
- Len Kendall and Daniel Honigman at the3six5 project
- Jeff Caswell at "Connect! Marketing in the Social Media Era"
- Raz Godelnik
- AIGA Portland's Sustainability Committee
- Melissa Delzio

Megan Strand would like to thank everyone who took the time to write or promote this book and specifically:

- Ted Strand
- Ron Johnson
- Carrie Gaines
- Peter Korchnak